EXTRAORDINARY RECIPES FROM

SALT LAKE CITY CHEF'S TABLE

BECKY AND JOSH ROSENTHAL

THE CROSSROADS OF THE WEST

gpp

GLOBE PEQUOT
Guilford, Connecticut

Globe Pequot is an imprint of Rowman & Littlefield

Distributed by NATIONAL BOOK NETWORK

Copyright © 2015 by Rowman & Littlefield

All photography by Josh & Becky Rosenthal.

British Library Cataloguing in Publication Information Available

Library of Congress Cataloging-in-Publication Data

Rosenthal, Becky, author.
  Salt Lake City chef's table : extraordinary recipes from the crossroads of the West / Josh & Becky Rosenthal.
    pages cm.
  ISBN 978-1-4930-0655-7 (hardback)
  1. Cooking, American—Western style. 2. Cooking—Utah—Salt Lake City. I. Rosenthal, Josh, author. II. Title.
  TX715.2.W47R74 2014
  641.59792'258—dc23

                                2014039134

ISBN 978-1-4930-1333-3 (ebook)

∞™ The paper used in this publication meets the minimum requirements of American National Standard for Information Sciences—Permanence of Paper for Printed Library Materials, ANSI/NISO Z39.48-1992.

Restaurants and chefs often come and go, and menus are ever changing. We recommend you call ahead to obtain current information before visiting any of the establishments in this book.

To Everett, our son, who happily joined us on this adventure, tasting all kinds of foods and meeting chefs and restaurant owners around the city, all before the age of one. We are grateful to have such a joyful boy who enjoys food as much as we do.

Contents

Acknowledgments

While we have many to thank, we must first say that this book would not have been possible without the many generous restaurant owners and chefs who graciously shared with us not only their stories but their beloved recipes as well.

To our little guy, Everett, who cheerfully endured long dinners and the restraint of high chairs, while we interviewed, photographed, and tasted.

To the many waiters and waitresses who patiently picked up Cheerios and supplied baby food as needed.

To our closest friends who gave us grace during this time that we weren't as available or attentive. Thanks also to the many of you who tested and tasted recipes—Dawn, Sandy, Christie, Annalise, Rachelle, Jordan, Julie, Lana, Matt, Haley, Heidi, Kelley, Tyler, Carol, Anne, Ashley, Josie, Craig, Amanda, and Debbie (who I haven't even met). Many of you went to multiple grocery stores, did research, and spent time converting recipes to home cook–friendly measurements. These recipes would be filled with chef jargon and shorthand without you!

From this adventure we'll keep with us fond memories of our family of three venturing out into the city to taste and listen to local restaurants' way of seasoning Salt Lake.

Those in the Salt Lake City dining scene form a community that is inspiring, and we will remember this experience by your generosity and care for one another and us.

Introduction

Though the West was won years and years ago, the pioneer spirit lives on in Salt Lake City (SLC). The local food scene is ripe with opportunity and alive with food entrepreneurs filled with ideas that many thought would never take off in Salt Lake City—let alone fly.

SLC's brand is better summed up by the Golden Spike connecting the Transcontinental Railroad than the culinary adventure that now defines the emerging urban food scene. The western myth of the cowboy riding into the sunset is alive and well here—only now the cowboy is just as likely to be a chef, and the opportunity formerly found in the elusive sunset is found on Main Street and State Street and all the neighborhoods clamoring for identities of their own.

This is the Salt Lake City food scene, a group of foodies leading the charge for a renewed city, serving everything from bone marrow to tumbleweed, foraging for mushrooms and new ideas to elevate the city and its culture.

As with any pioneer-spirited place and mentality, the future is bright with hope. Salt Lake City deserves recognition for its innovation at the chef's table, the barman's bar, or the sommelier's cellar. For years the tourists have come for the world's greatest snow, and rightly so. But now the adventure seekers are pleased to find food on par with the great cities of America. Some would say that the state color is orange for all the construction cones and signs downtown. The massive awakening of food culture boosts our economy as well as our palates.

The pioneer spirit lends itself well to generous collaboration in the great Salt Lake City. Restaurant owners and chefs approached this project with open hands, offering us more food, more recipes, and more story than we had space to put in these pages. Not only did neighborhood restaurant owners open their doors to us, but they also made sure we knew of their neighbors so they could be featured in the book too. On our visit to Alamexo, Chef Matthew Lake made sure we knew that Ryan Lowder's latest endeavor, Copper Common, was on par with his already successful local staple the Copper Onion, a must-visit for us. Steven Rosenberg from Liberty Heights Fresh told us that no book about the SLC dining scene is complete without a trip to meet Scott Evans of Pago and Finca fame. In fact, many restaurant owners told us that Scott is one of the best guys to work with in the industry.

The state of the food scene here is marked by this type of generosity and pioneering nature. Comprised in these pages is a snapshot of the scene as we saw it as we wrote this book. Things are changing rapidly, and new restaurants spring up regularly. But these new restaurants would never have found their place without a few names that have gone before them. Similarly, the state of the scene today is influencing a meaningful movement told only in the future tense.

Steven Rosenberg, Pioneer

Utahans regularly use the word "pioneer." We even celebrate the day the pioneers came down through Emigration Canyon with handcarts (conveniently called Pioneer Day). It carries a lot of weight in Utah and is not to be used or taken lightly.

Perhaps in light of this, it sounds a bit sensational to call Steven Rosenberg a pioneer. It's not. Steven is one of the few food business owners who survived the last twenty years, who pushed for better food and better ingredients then, and who continues to be out in front of food trends now, still advocating for better food and better ingredients. He opened Liberty Heights Fresh in 1993 when Utah's idea of locally grown, locally owned, and fresh had died off with the pioneers of the previous century. At the time, his operation served only fresh produce and flowers.

If the present condition of Utah is exciting, it's because of the groundwork of people like Steven, who worked hard to help Utah tell a better story about itself by putting great producers and food entrepreneurs on display in every way possible.

Copper Onion, Today

Copper Onion likely sees the most patrons of any locally owned restaurant in town. For a place that's always packed, always hustling, they've achieved something few can maintain at their size—quality.

The success that Ryan Lowder experiences at Copper Onion tells a lot of other timid potential entrepreneurs that perhaps a quality local restaurant with a top-notch chef and uncompromised wine list can succeed in Utah. Ryan Lowder and the rest of the restaurateurs in his class have all confidently and capably pushed our city over the hump from seeming culinary insignificance to a place other culinary capitals are watching. Not that we've arrived yet, but there is a groundswell. Salt Lake City is working hard to achieve its own identity. It's not a version of Portland or San Francisco. It's Salt Lake City, storied warts and all.

Ryan Lowder embraced Salt Lake City and aided in elevating it.

Church and State Spirits, Our Future

Yes, another strong statement about something entirely unknown. I don't mean to put so much pressure on Scott Gardner, Sean Neves, and Matt Pfohl. In fact, let me remove it quickly. These individuals are not the future of Utah, but the way they think, operate, and interact is the future of Utah. They embody the future that most SLC urban dwellers prefer, one that pushes to think differently about everything. But the new ideas they bring to the table aren't those of innovation. No, they're actually those that call us to simply embrace what tastes good in an environment that feels right.

Church and State Spirits is a group of three guys committed to great spirit-based beverages. And they'll search long and hard to find these beverages and present them in a way that encourages you to drink them. This explanation sounds overly distilled, but it's really not. The art of taking something world-class and opening it up to the masses to enjoy is a gift. You don't have to be an expert to love something made by these guys. But if you are a connoisseur, pay close attention and you'll see them shake hands with every devil in the details.

We think that's where Utah is leaning now: accessible meets master craftsmanship. Thanks to Steven Rosenberg, a foundation was laid for creative experts to find quality food in Utah. Thanks to Copper Onion, Utah believes in itself. Both of these pioneers laid the foundation for Church and State Spirits and similar-minded food entrepreneurs to blow the top off what's possible in Utah.

The soul of this book tells the stories of people wanting something to be proud of and finding it in the dining room seats of Utah's latest version of pioneers.

SALT LAKE CITY FOOD EVENTS

Salt Lake City and the greater Salt Lake area are host to several incredible food events. We mark our calendars every year to make sure we can attend all of our favorites.

- Save a summer evening in June to attend Park City's Savor the Summit, when restaurants move all their tables to the center of Main Street, creating one long communal table and an incredible evening of food and drink.

- In the fall, Caputo's Market puts on The Chocolate Festival, showcasing chocolate creations from all the best chefs in town.

- Tastemakers, a two-day progressive dinner hosted by *Salt Lake Magazine*, is a great time to taste many of the best downtown Salt Lake restaurants.

- Celebrate the Bounty, Local First's annual benefit, features Utah's finest fare from local producers.

- Oktoberfest at Snowbird pairs an incredible mountain scene with tall steins of local brews, as well as brats loaded with sauerkraut.

- Red, White & Snow Vintner Dinners, small dinner parties in Park City with great wine and food, have become a most enjoyable way to raise money for the National Ability Center.

- The annual Greek Festival, in September, has had as many as 50,000 visitors during its three-day experience. The classic gyro is especially good, but don't miss out on the more unusual items, like the *tyropita*, a cheese triangle wrapped in flaky phyllo pastry; the *stifado*, a spiced beef stew with pearl onions; and the *loukoumades*, addicting honey-soaked donuts.

Meals in Salt Lake City

Appetizers

Whether it's an appetizer or small plate, chefs create this course with special attention. Salads are anything but a pile of flavorless greens with cheap dressing and average cheese. Meat plates are certainly not ordinary, designed with locally made cheese, salami, and preserves, and are enjoying great national attention.

At Finca you can make a meal by ordering and passing around small plates of tasty bites, from smoked chicken croquettes to shishito peppers. It's the best way to try it all and have an extended meal with good friends, the kind who don't mind if you all plunge your forks into the same dish.

You won't be able to pass the appetizer course at places like Fresco, Alamexo, or Pago as the options are just too tempting. Polenta with wild mushrooms and pomodoro, table-side guacamole spiced to your liking, and a tasting of carrots (raw, pickled, confit, and pureed with mascarpone) are just a few starters worth your attention.

Breakfasts

Breakfast is a meal celebrated in Salt Lake. Some take it with a mug of hot coffee, others with a tall glass of fresh-squeezed juice. Morning aficionados will find waffles made the way they used to in Bruges, huevos with house-made tomatillo salsa and farm-fresh eggs, rich hollandaise atop bacon and avocado, baked goods to give you a taste of France, and pancakes so dreamy and fluffy you may just give up making them at home.

On any given weekend or weekday morning, you'll find a seemingly cheerful line out the door at Park Cafe. If you drive by 300 South near Pioneer Park, you'll see folks lining down the street to get a crispy caramelized Bruges Waffle. And if you hope to hit up one of the favorite local bakeries like Tulie for a Morning Bun or Les Madeleines for a Kouing Aman, we'll just say you better get there a little early.

Salt Lake City living, whether you're a skier or a city dweller, requires a good breakfast.

Desserts

Salt Lake diners are powerless when it comes to desserts. From ice cream and gelato to elegant layered cakes and soufflés, desserts are the more common vice, whereas other large cities may have a stronger penchant for mixed drinks and full-bodied wines.

We live in a city where small cookie shops are worth fighting for, secret pastry recipes are prized and sometimes challenged, and ice cream shops are the most popular date destinations.

Amber Billingsly's Butterscotch Budino perfectly follows any Italian meal at Vinto; Kelly Sue Pugh's creativity is seen in her layered carrot cake served in mason jars or her homemade Ho Hos. And one visit to Jean Gorge's grand pastry case at Gourmandise will certainly not be enough.

The locals' appetite for dessert is well matched with valley chefs' ability to invent sweet post-meal pleasures.

Entrees

Though small plates and desserts are currently hogging the spotlight in Salt Lake dining, entrees are anything but ignored. Local chefs fully embrace the freedoms of Salt Lake's nonjudgmental restaurant scene to create fabulous dishes with local, seasonal, and quality ingredients.

While some larger dining cities are competitive and thus restrictive, Salt Lake proves to be one where risks are celebrated and creativity runs deep. We can't forget that we live in the Wild West.

Tyler Stokes at Lugano pairs cauliflower with pancetta on top of spaghetti; Em's turns shredded cabbage into creamy fettuccine, and beef stroganoff has never been so elegant and tasty than at Copper Onion.

Mexican entrees are well worth their price tags at Alamexo and Frida Bistro.

Thai curry, *pho*, and Indian masala are made naturally with fresh ingredients. Try the MSG-free *pho* at Oh Mai or the Gang Dang Curry filled with crisp veggies at Chanon Thai.

The entrees chefs create around the valley are one of the reasons Salt Lake is such a great city to live in.

Beverages

A handful of great bartenders, distillers, wine makers, sommeliers, and restaurant managers are changing the complexion of drinking in Utah. There's something of an awakening for responsible, sophisticated drinkers more interested in the taste of their beverage than the effects of it. Sure, the head-lightening effects of a few good drinks are welcomed after a long week, but largely the new culture cares to know the difference between tequila and mezcal or what makes vermouth from France different from vermouth from Italy.

A culture demanding good booze is growing in Utah with some very capable hands at the helm. Church and State Spirits (Scott Gardner from Finca, Matt Pfohl from Pallet, and Sean Neves, the lone wolf bluetooth ringleader) along with the Bar X crew and a few others tell a story about Utah by way of mixed drink, another evolving chapter in the state's culinary scene.

Bar X came along at a time when Utah needed a good drink. The prevalent well gin and tonics and Jack and Cokes belong more to a fraternity party than an evening on the town. The owners of Bar X took something really old (Bar X first began operation in 1933) and made it relevant again. The bar menu offers just about any cocktail from a bygone era and, with the same modus operandi, made it worth $9 a drink.

Bar X (re)opened its doors when just about every restaurant with a bit of creativity and entrepreneurial spirit could be a first of some kind. The first whiskey distillery, High West (post Valley Tan). The first drinking chocolate, Mezzo. The first artisan salami maker, Creminelli. The list goes on and on. To some a $9 drink is an insult. Why would Bar X charge so much for such a small quantity of beverage? The owners chose to elevate the cocktail scene and take a price-point risk, and Utah embraced it fully. In some armchair

sociological and psychological terms, Bar X communicated to Utahans that they're worth a $9 cocktail. It feels good to be worth a $9 cocktail.

In Utah we find our way around strange liquor laws and even come to celebrate them in a sense. While most of the unusual liquor laws have been done away with, one remains: You must order food with your drink if you're having alcohol at a restaurant. Twist our arm. I guess we'll have to pull up a chair at the bar and stay awhile. Some of the best foods are served at the places where you can get a good cocktail.

Sit at the bar at Copper Onion and you'll get to see most of your food prepared. Their ricotta dumplings or the braised pork belly make great small bites to go along with one of their signature drinks.

At Pallet, dessert and drinks are a favored combo. The bar is lined with industrial lighting and rustic bar stools, a comfortable spot for a late-night date.

Sip sake while you watch how the masters make incredibly intricate sushi rolls at the bar at Naked Fish.

And you may be able to chat with the chef or sommelier at Pago if you get a spot at its bar.

ALAMEXO

268 SOUTH STATE STREET
SALT LAKE CITY, UTAH 84111
(801) 779-4747
ALAMEXO.COM
MATTHEW LAKE, CHEF/OWNER

Alamexo embodies a hybrid of Chef Matthew Lake's past and Salt Lake City's future. Whether it's Mezzo Chocolate, Red Iguana, the slew of taco carts, or Frida Bistro, Salt Lake City is interested in Mexican tradition with an elevated twist as well as a traditional emphasis.

Salt Lake City continues to build its food credibility by importing great chefs. Enter Matthew Lake and his Mexican concept, Alamexo. Many of the great chefs who make SLC a destination for foodies cut their teeth and sharpened their knives in other cities. There's no shame in it. Every city has its story, and Salt Lake City's is partially a tale of culinary experts finding a home among the urban/mountain setting and making their mark after time spent at other culinary destinations.

Chef Matthew Lake comes to town by way of some of the best East Coast eateries, learning from some of the best chefs around. In 1996, while working at New Heights in Washington, DC, Matt won *Food & Wine*'s prestigious Best New Chef award. Before his westward trek, Lake was in the kitchen at Rosa Mexicana with Josefina Howard, learning the nuance and craft of contemporary Mexican food.

Needless to say, Matt brings a pedigree to Salt Lake City that legitimizes Alamexo (and really anything he attempts).

Bright Mexican colors combined with clean modern lines proclaim a traditional Mexican-meets-fine-dining melting pot that comes together cleanly after a quick look at the menu—table-side guacamole (fresh guacamole prepared by the server in front of the patrons), Enchiladas Suizas (roasted pulled chicken seasoned with epazote, baked in a tomatillo cream salsa topped with melted queso Chihuahua, cilantro, and white onion), and a selection of twenty tequilas to match the flavors waiting in the kitchen. Something intentional and rich with tradition is happening within the walls of Alamexo.

Take a drive down State Street and you'll pass the city's heirlooms that will be around for years to come—Eagle Gate, the state capitol, the city building—but don't miss the places like Alamexo that are changing the face of the city. Juxtaposed against the staples, Alamexo is a bite of freshness in a city falsely stereotyped for the opposite.

Enchiladas Suizas

(SERVES 4)

For the salsa verde con crema por suizas:

16 (64 ounces) tomatillos, washed and peeled

5 jalapeños, roasted and stems removed

3 ounces garlic cloves

1 bunch cilantro

½ cup vegetable oil

Salt to taste

½ cup heavy cream

For the enchiladas:

Lard or vegetable oil

8 (6-inch) corn tortillas

1 whole (3-pound) chicken, roasted and shredded, seasoned with fresh epazote

16 ounces salsa verde (see recipe)

12 ounces Chihuahua cheese, grated

1 white onion, minced

1 bunch cilantro, chopped

To make the salsa verde con crema por suizas: Start by boiling the tomatillos until soft. Blend the tomatillos, jalapeños, garlic, and cilantro in a blender until smooth, leaving behind a few speckles. Fry the sauce in the oil, then let simmer for 45 minutes. Salt to taste and finish with cream. Cool and store.

To prepare the enchiladas: Preheat oven to broil. Put a spoonful of lard (or vegetable oil) in a 10-inch skillet and heat. When the lard or oil is hot, put the tortillas in one at a time and sear for 5 seconds on each side. Remove from the skillet and place on an oven pan.

Put 4 ounces of chicken into each tortilla and roll into an enchilada. Place all eight enchiladas in the oven pan and cover completely with the *salsa verde con crema por suizas*. Top with the Chihuahua cheese.

Cook the enchiladas in the oven for 3–4 minutes or until the cheese is light brown. Top with minced onion and finish with chopped cilantro.

Amour Spreads

AmourSpreads.com
John and Casee Francis, Owners

Take the wrong turn while on a hike in the beautiful Utah mountains and you might end up in a field of thimbleberries. Better still, you may end up altering your career path to preserve the memory of the berries you found that day. John and Casee Francis did just that and now find themselves lost in a love affair with marmalade and jam.

The Francises can now be found in fruit-stained aprons gazing over their bubbling French copper pots filled with the freshest fruits of the season. Either that, or you will find them at bustling Utah farmers' markets, handing silver spoons to new friends, giving them a taste of what they have lovingly created by hand.

Amour Spreads preserves the old style of jam making, adding only the basics to maintain the real, ripe flavor of the fruits. Pure cane sugar, freshly squeezed lemon juice, and fresh fruit are the only ingredients you'll find on their labels, plus a few herbs depending on the desired flavor profile.

One taste of John and Casee's creations and you'll be hunting down ulterior uses for what's in the jar. It's too good to only experience in traditional settings. Try the jams swirled in plain Greek yogurt, over braised meats, in cocktails or hors d'oeuvres, in the thumbprints of your cookies, whisked into salad dressings, or on top of rich creamy brie.

The love and care in each jar transcends what you put in your mouth. Ask John about his desire to grow the business and you'll see someone motivated by getting real ingredients into folks' homes, but with an endearing hesitancy to not let the business grow *too* much for the danger of losing what makes it special—quality, handmade jams and marmalades created and served with a relational touch.

On their behalf (and very much so on ours), we'd like to thank Scott Evans from Pago for helping launch this quality product and Steven Rosenberg from Liberty Heights Fresh for continually promoting Armour Spreads.

This won't be a jar living on your shelf for long like many other jams.

SAVORY JAM, GREENS, AND CHEESE CROSTINI

(SERVES 4–6)

Olive oil

2 cloves garlic, diced

2 bunches kale (laminate kale, green kale, red kale, or combo), washed, stems removed, and chopped coarsely

Salt

1 fresh baguette, sliced into ½-inch rounds

1 clove garlic, whole

1 jar of jam (Amour Spreads Savory Heirloom Tomato Jam is recommended.)

⅛ pound cheese, thinly sliced (Beehive Promontory or Seahive is recommended.)

To prepare kale: Pour several good glugs of olive oil into a large pot on medium heat, then add the diced garlic and sauté for 1 minute. Add chopped kale and a pinch of salt to taste.

Stir, then cover and cook. After 4 minutes, remove lid, stir again, then re-cover for 4 additional minutes. Remove from heat and set aside. Once slightly cooled, dice the greens to medium fine.

To prepare crostini: Lightly brush baguette rounds on one side with olive oil and toast in the oven or boiler for approximately 2–4 minutes until lightly browned. Remove rounds from the oven and, while warm, gently rub tops with the whole garlic clove.

To assemble: Spread each toasted baguette round with Amour Spreads Savory Heirloom Tomato Jam, then add a layer of sliced cheese to each jammy baguette round. Top with a teaspoon full of diced kale.

Serve immediately or at room temperature. Can be prepared up to 1 hour prior to serving.

Avenues Bistro

564 East Third Avenue
Salt Lake City, Utah 84103
(801) 831-5409
Kathie Chadbourne, Owner
Kelly Sue Pugh, Pastry Chef
Eric Daniels, Head Chef

Drawing on her love for the neighborhood and the community that surrounds it, Kathie Chadbourne brought a little bistro to town. "The Avenues Bistro was built by and for the community," says Kathie. Literally, the neighborhood came out to help wash windows and lay flooring. No loans were drawn from banks, and no interest accrued; the restaurant was funded primarily by friends, family, and Kathie herself as she sold everything she had to invest in her dream. "This is the power of a neighborhood being hungry for a community gathering place."

The love of food and local product all come together in this little bistro. No processed foods are used, and the old-fashioned way of enjoying conversation around a table is ensured. The Avenues Bistro is a true urban garden-to-table restaurant. Out back are chicken coops, strawberry gardens, and rows of herbs and vegetables. Lining the walls of the interior you'll find last year's produce preserved in tall jars, cookbooks all speaking to simple, seasonal cooking methods, and shiny rocks gathered from around the state. This earthy atmosphere connects guests to the land on which they reside.

Two chefs take pride in their work at Avenues Bistro. Kelly Sue Pugh, Kathie's daughter, shares her creative juices in the pastry arena, while Eric Daniels makes use of the garden produce for the regular menu items and specials. Talent and passion are evident in both chefs as they enjoy working for such a community-centered cafe. Eric has been won over by the fresh ingredients he gets to use in his brunch menu, such

as the huevos rancheros and the grass-fed beef for the house burger, which he was hesitant about at first but now loves. Kelly enjoys the reality that working with her mom means having freedom to make unique pastries like homemade Ho Hos, carrot cake in mason jars, and beautifully layered opera cake.

The business is now hitting its sweet spot as Kathie and her crew share their kitchen creations with everyone who was so generous with them. It's too bad that Kathie's approach is so novel these days. Avenues Bistro better resembles the old days and a beautiful ideal.

CARROT CAKE

(SERVES 12)

For the cake:

3 cups all-purpose flour

1 teaspoon salt

1 tablespoon baking soda

1 tablespoon cinnamon

1 tablespoon ground ginger

4 eggs

2 cups sugar

1½ cups oil (olive oil)

1 tablespoon vanilla extract

1 vanilla bean

1 cup peeled and shredded carrot (about 2 large carrots)

For the vanilla bean icing:

1 vanilla bean

1 cup heavy cream

2 pounds cream cheese

1 cup sugar

1 tablespoon vanilla extract

To prepare the cake: Preheat oven to 350°F and grease a 13 x 9-inch cake pan or two 9-inch round pans.

Sift all dry ingredients, flour to ginger, in a medium bowl. In a mixer beat eggs, sugar, oil, and vanilla. Slit the vanilla bean lengthwise and scrape out the seeds into the egg mixture. Beat the egg/sugar mixture until it doubles in size. With a spatula, fold in dry ingredients, then fold in carrots.

Bake at 350°F for 45 minutes or until a toothpick comes out clean. Let cool, then frost with vanilla bean icing.

To prepare the icing: Using a paring knife, slit the vanilla bean lengthwise and scrape out the vanilla beans into the heavy cream. Discard the vanilla bean (or save for another use). Combine all ingredients in a food processor or blender and blend until smooth.

To serve in jars, bake cake as directed then break up cake into smaller pieces. Layer in jars, alternating cake with frosting.

AVENUES BISTRO HUEVOS RANCHEROS

(SERVES 4)

Salsa rojo (see recipe)

Salsa verde (see recipe)

Refried black beans (see recipe)

12 homemade corn tortillas (see recipe)

1 cup grated cheddar cheese

4 eggs

1 cup arugula

For the salsa rojo:

1 cup diced onions

3 cloves garlic, chopped

4 roasted tomatoes

2 tablespoons chili powder

2 teaspoons oregano

1 tablespoon cumin

2 tablespoons butter

Salt to taste

To prepare salsa rojo: In a medium saucepan, sauté onions until golden brown. Add garlic and cook for about a minute, then add tomatoes and 1 cup water. Bring to a simmer over medium heat, then add spices and simmer for about 10 minutes.

Using a blender or immersion blender, blend, then add butter and salt to taste.

For the salsa verde:

6 fresh tomatillos, roasted

1 cup diced onions

3 cloves garlic, chopped

6 Anaheim peppers, roasted

2 teaspoons oregano

1 tablespoon cumin

Salt to taste

To roast tomatillos: Preheat oven broiler. Remove husks from tomatillos and rinse under warm water to remove stickiness. Broil fresh tomatillos on rack of a broiler pan 1–2 inches from heat, turning once, until tomatillos are softened and slightly charred, about 7 minutes.

To prepare salsa verde: In a medium saucepan, sauté onions until golden brown. Add garlic and cook for about a minute.

Add tomatillos, Anaheim peppers, and 1 cup water. Bring to a simmer over medium heat, then add spices and simmer for about 10 minutes.

Using a blender or immersion blender, blend, then add salt to taste.

For the refried black beans:

1 cup diced onions
1 tablespoon butter
3 cloves garlic, chopped
1 jalapeño, diced
4 cups black beans, soaked overnight
1 tablespoon cumin
Salt to taste

Sauté onions in butter until golden. Add garlic and jalapeño and cook for about a minute.

Add beans and 3 quarts water. Bring to a boil, then lower heat to a simmer and cook until the beans are soft.

Drain off any excess water. Mash the beans with a potato masher. Season with cumin and salt to taste.

For the corn tortillas:

1¾ cups masa harina
1⅛ cups water

In a medium bowl mix together masa harina and hot water until thoroughly combined. Turn dough onto a clean surface and knead until pliable and smooth. If dough is too sticky, add more masa harina; if it begins to dry out, sprinkle with water. Cover dough tightly with plastic wrap and allow to stand for 30 minutes.

Preheat a cast-iron skillet or griddle to medium-high. Divide dough into fifteen equal-size balls. Using a tortilla press, a rolling pin, or your hands, press each ball of dough flat between two sheets of plastic wrap.

Immediately place tortilla in preheated pan and allow to cook for approximately 30 seconds or until browned and slightly puffy. Turn tortilla over to brown on the other side for approximately 30 seconds more, then transfer to a plate. Repeat process with each ball of dough. Keep tortillas covered with a towel to stay warm and moist until ready to serve

To assemble the huevos rancheros: Fry the eggs in butter or oil on medium-high heat until whites are firm and not runny. On four individual plates layer a tortilla, a smear of black beans, a tortilla, a smear of black beans, and a tortilla. Spoon a few tablespoons of salsa rojo on half of the plate and a few tablespoons of salsa verde on the other half. Top the salsa on each plate with ¼ cup grated cheddar then one fried egg. Garnish with arugula.

Beehive Cheese

2440 East 6600 South, #8
Uintah, Utah 84405
(801) 476-0900
BEEHIVECHEESE.COM
Pat Ford and Tim Welsh, Owners

Pat Ford says cheese is the next wine renaissance, and after hearing a little more about the current studies on cheese in America, it's easy to believe. Artisan cheese consumption has recently doubled, and 70 percent of those artisan cheese lines began after 2005. "Cheese just kept rearing its head," says Pat as he and his brother in law, Tim Welsh, considered entering into the artisan food world away from corporate America.

With this family business Pat and Tim sought a simpler life to better enjoy their families and Utah's beautiful outdoors. The idea of a simple life making cheese changed as their cheese company quickly grew into a cheese empire. They still strive to keep business in the family; both their sons work as cheesemakers and run specialty food events for the company. Those in the company who are not connected by blood have become like family as well.

And the cause of all this success, Pat says, is "A good product and strong relationships. People like buying goods from businesses they like, but of course the

product must be good first." He is proud of the cheese they're creating, which financially and literally sustains his family. Cheese omelets, grilled cheese panini, and mac and cheese greet the family at the table every week.

While most of their cheese lines begin with Promontory, a nutty and fruity blend of cheddar, each variety is quite unique and creative. Barely Buzzed, a favorite around the country, is rubbed with lavender and coffee. SeaHive has a layer of sea salt and local honey, Big John's Cajun is bursting with Cajun spices, and Beehive Fresh is similar to a mozzarella. Cheese curds and RUSK crackers carry the Beehive brand as well.

As artisan cheese excitement grows in America, it will continue to grow in this family, making those of us in Utah proud.

Aggiano Potato Artichoke Gratin

(SERVES 8–12)

3 large leeks

2 tablespoons butter

Salt and pepper to taste

1 (14-ounce) can artichokes (not marinated), drained

1 tablespoon Dijon mustard

8 ounces Beehive Aggiano cheese, grated

2 large russet potatoes

1 cup heavy cream

Preheat oven to 350°F. Slice green tops off leeks and cut lengthwise. Soak in water to clean thoroughly and then thinly slice. In a medium sauté pan over medium heat, melt butter and add leeks. Salt and pepper to taste. Cook for 5 minutes, stirring occasionally to prevent browning. Take off heat and add artichokes and mustard. Mix thoroughly. Cool slightly, then stir in three-quarters of the cheese.

Using a food processor slicing disk or mandoline, thinly slice potatoes, then transfer to a large bowl and add cold water to cover. Stir with your hands to rinse slices, then drain well. Layer potatoes between paper towels and pat dry.

Layer one-third of the potato slices in the bottom of a lightly buttered 9 x 13-inch casserole dish, overlapping slightly. Sprinkle with salt and pepper. Evenly spoon half of the leek-cheese mixture over the top. Add a second layer of potatoes, salt, and pepper, then the remaining leek-cheese mixture, then a final layer of potatoes. Slowly pour cream over the top. (Cream should come up about three-quarters to the top of the potato mixture.) Top with remaining cheese.

Cover casserole with foil, being careful not to press the foil too close to the cheese topping. Cook covered for 40 minutes, until cheese melts. Uncover and continue to cook until potatoes are tender and cheese is brown, about 20 more minutes. Serve warm.

CHEESE

While Beehive Cheese remains the most nationally known cheese coming out of Utah, it's by far not the only cheese worth recognition.

Heber Valley Cheese offers their unique *juustoleipa*, which is best toasted and served warm. You need no additions to make this cheese into a great party appetizer.

Drake Family Farms offers fresh goat milk cheese, while Gold Creek Farms and Rockhill Creamery make cheese with milk from their unique Brown Swiss cows.

Black Sheep Cafe

19 North University Avenue
Provo, Utah 84601
(801) 607-2485
BLACKSHEEPCAFE.COM
Bleu Adams, Owner
Mark Daniel Mason, Head Chef

Similar to the term *black sheep*, the Black Sheep Cafe may seem a bit odd or seemingly out of place when it comes to dining in Provo. We mean that in the best way. The Black Sheep's peculiarity lends well to its draw. This truly family-run establishment takes Native American cuisine and honorably serves it in a new fashion.

The owner, Bleu Adams, manages the restaurant while her mom is in the kitchen making the prized family fry bread recipe and her brother wears the white hat of the head chef.

Bleu's family is from a Navajo reservation in Arizona, where she spent much of her years as a teenager. Her hope is to keep her heritage alive by passing on some of her culture's most delicious foods to Utah, which she now calls home. She started with a small food cart, all the while dreaming of one day owning a restaurant. In fact, she saved for six years so that she could start this restaurant without even taking out a loan. She epitomizes commitment and determination when it comes to accomplishing her dreams.

The signature dish of the Black Sheep Cafe, Navajo tacos, comes heaping with fresh ingredients like spiced pinto beans, tender slow-cooked beef, or pork smothered in green chile sauce. And the traditional fry bread—good luck getting this recipe; not even Bleu knows it—is just as amazing as it's hyped to be. If you're not up for tacos, there are plenty of other choices on the menu to satisfy, from posole to enchiladas, all made in the Navajo tradition with a modern twist.

While favorites from the entree menu are varied, diners agree on dessert: Orange Habanero Crème Brûlée. The cafe takes this seemingly common French dessert and turns it up a notch with citrus flavor and a kick of pepper—not too hot to deter the Utah crowds, of course.

Black Sheep Cafe's Southwest Caprese

(SERVES 4)

1 red bell pepper
1 yellow bell pepper
1 Anaheim chile
1 teaspoon vegetable oil
8 medium basil leaves
½ cup extra-virgin olive oil
1 teaspoon coarse black pepper
1½ pounds fresh mozzarella

1 teaspoon liquid smoke
4 Roma tomatoes
8 yellow cherry tomatoes (may substitute red cherry tomatoes)
1 teaspoon smoked salt (may substitute kosher salt)
4 large basil leaves
1 tablespoon vegetable oil
2 teaspoons balsamic vinegar

Wash and dry red and yellow bell peppers and Anaheim chile. Place peppers and chile in a medium mixing bowl and coat with 1 teaspoon vegetable oil.

Roast peppers and chile on a grill or under the broiler until blistered and blackened slightly on all sides. Remove to a bowl and cover with plastic wrap to seal. Allow to steam until cool enough to handle, approximately 20 minutes. Remove skins, stems, and seeds (do not rinse). Slice peppers and chile into long, thin strips.

Place peppers and chile in a medium mixing bowl. Stack four medium basil leaves and cut into very thin strips. Add basil to peppers and chile with the extra-virgin olive oil and coarse black pepper. Mix well and cover. Refrigerate for half an hour to overnight.

Slice mozzarella into sixteen ¼-inch-thick round medallions. Place mozzarella in a bowl and cover with cold water and liquid smoke and set aside.

Slice each Roma tomato into four medallions, discarding small end pieces, and set aside. Cut eight cherry tomatoes in half and set aside. Stack four remaining medium basil leaves and cut into thin strips and set aside.

On a working plate lay flat four tomato slices and four mozzarella slices. Sprinkle slices with smoked salt to taste.

Alternately stack four slices each of the tomatoes and mozzarella in a rainbow pattern on a serving plate. Place a mound of peppers and chiles under the rainbow. Place four halves of cherry tomatoes on the plate, then top the pepper mound with one-quarter of the sliced basil. Place the stem side of one large basil leaf at the base of the peppers. Drizzle plate with extra-virgin olive oil. Drizzle tomatoes and mozzarella with balsamic vinegar to taste.

Repeat with remaining three plates.

BLUE PLATE DINER

2041 SOUTH 2100 EAST
SALT LAKE CITY, UTAH 84108
(801) 463-1151
JOHN BOUZEK, OWNER

People only complain about one thing at the Blue Plate Diner: the wait to get a seat. This diner is the choice spot of Sugar House residents. Located just blocks from Sugar House Park and near the highway, its easy access may be its only downfall.

Blue Plate offers both traditional and untraditional breakfast fare, attracting pretty much any demographic nearby, from a crowd of firemen to a hipster vegan couple living down the street. On the traditional side their corned beef hash is a favorite, made with brined corned beef that's been boiled and sliced thin in-house. The beef is served tender, almost crisp, and topped with cheese, fried eggs, and a side of toast. Rye pairs well, if you are looking for recommendations.

For more classics, try the Classic Blue, house Benedict, or any omelet.

After that, things get a little more trendy. The menu includes five variations of Benedict, from the SMA (spinach, mushroom, and avocado) to the country Benedict with smoked ham, buttermilk biscuits, and country gravy. Pancakes come in a variety to choose from as well, from vegan pancakes to country corn cakes, all with your choice of fruit, nuts, coconut, or chocolate chips. The corn cakes are especially good, with a little more texture than traditional pancakes and the flavor of cornbread. Try them with blueberries for a real treat. The tofu vegetable scramble and vegan tofu breakfast burrito satisfy the vegan crowd, while the pork chili verde burrito and the huevos rancheros satisfy those walking in extra hungry.

The vibe is just as funky as some of the menu items, with

vintage decor salvaged from around Utah, including its soda fountain built in 1949. The diner is even older than some of the random objects lined up above the bar, as it was built around the turn of the twentieth century.

Blue Plate doesn't just fill a niche in Salt Lake, it fills every seat, the whole neighborhood, and beyond with exactly what anyone would want in a comfort food diner. Perhaps they do it too well.

BLUE PLATE VEGAN BURGER PATTY

(SERVES 4–6)

2½ cups black beans
2½ cups garbanzo beans
½ cup raw old-fashioned oatmeal
½ cup water
1 cup finely chopped white onion
1 cup finely chopped celery
1½ teaspoons salt
¾ teaspoon black pepper
½ teaspoon granulated onion (or ¼ teaspoon onion powder)
½ teaspoon granulated garlic (or ¼ teaspoon garlic powder)
1 tablespoon chili powder
3 cups panko bread crumbs
½ cup all-purpose flour

Coarsely puree the black beans and garbanzo beans. Bring raw oats and water to a boil and cook for five minutes. Add oats and all other ingredients to the beans. Let cool for 10 minutes then mix by hand. Measure out 5-ounce portions and smash to flatten into patties. Brown both sides in a pan with oil. Serve with a vegan bun, green leaf lettuce, sliced red onion, and tomato.

PANCAKES

This city loves its pancakes. And we have a wide variety, from lemon pancakes at the Lazy Day Cafe to the fluffy pancakes that live up to their nickname: "Heavenly Hotcakes."

Here are some words of wisdom on pancakes in Salt Lake City:

Go to the Park Cafe for pancakes the size of your head. Choose from buttermilk or multigrain, then blueberry or banana. A pancake sandwich is also a fun find here.

Drive up the Big Cottonwood Canyon to Silver Fork Lodge for their famous sourdough pancakes made with a sourdough starter over fifty years old.

The lemon pancakes at Lazy Day Cafe have a cult following and are served with their house-made buttermilk syrup.

Penny Anne's is like visiting your grandma's house—that is, if your grandma has the best recipe for fluffy pancakes. Pancake lovers and haters enjoy a short stack here.

Oasis Cafe serves up a grand German pancake with blueberry compote, worth sharing if you want something savory too.

Vertical Diner has a variety of vegetarian and gluten-free pancakes including raspberry and chocolate chip.

For a more unique hotcake, try the cinnamon roll pancake at Faustina, the cornmeal pancake at Blue Plate Diner, or Caribbean pancakes from Caffe Niche.

For a classic diner stack, hit up the Coachman's or The Original Pancake House.

CAFFE NICHE

779 EAST BROADWAY
SALT LAKE CITY, UTAH 84102
(801) 433-3380
CAFFENICHE.COM
ETHAN LAPPE, HEAD CHEF

Ethan Lappe, the chef at Caffe Niche, serves up one of the most enjoyed brunches in the city, and he does so in an accessible and easy fashion. While the egg sandwich is hard to resist, the menu is filled with great finds.

Their weekend brunch includes blackened fresh fish tacos, literally caught just days before serving, steak and eggs with sliced hanger steak, and kobe corned beef hash that keeps other chefs around town on their toes.

Chef Ethan Lappe was led to the kitchen out of a love for golf. At the age of twelve his wallet sat empty in his pocket, but by some cosmic cruelty he loved a rich man's sport, golf. With a small allowance and a sizable addiction to golf, he found a job as a short-order cook at a golf course. Until age seventeen he worked at various golf course kitchens, enjoying free golf all the while. These days, his time on the course is rare compared to his time in the kitchen.

At home Ethan enjoys using fresh ingredients and abstains from butter in his kitchen. At Niche he follows a similar rule, only using butter for a few dishes as he strives for a healthier menu. His hollandaise is made with extra-virgin olive oil and lemon juice, something he learned from a master chef, and his eggs are cooked in grape seed oil, which comes with a higher smoke point, but more importantly, a bit of nutritional value.

Weekday breakfast includes steel-cut organic oats, blueberries, toasted coconut, and a generous drizzle of local honey. The breakfast sandwich (the one that's hard *not* to order) is assembled with a house-made English muffin, perfectly scrambled eggs, thick slices of avocado, and bacon topped with Ethan's perfect hollandaise sauce.

While breakfast is definitely the most important meal of the day at Caffe Niche, the other mealtimes should not be ignored. Lunch includes fish tacos, Utah elk burger with chimichurri, and a roasted beet and arugula salad, to name a few.

From the fish to the eggs, Caffe Niche boasts, and rightly so, of the freshness of their food.

Caffe Niche Breakfast Sandwich

(SERVES 2)

For the sandwich:

2 house-made English muffins (see recipe)

2 scrambled eggs

1½ pieces bacon

¼ avocado

Hollandaise sauce (see recipe)

For the English muffins:

½ cup nonfat powdered milk

1 tablespoon sugar

1 teaspoon salt, divided

1 tablespoon shortening

1 cup hot water

1 envelope dry yeast

⅛ teaspoon sugar

⅓ cup warm water

2 cups all-purpose flour, sifted

Nonstick vegetable spray

For the hollandaise:

4 egg yolks

¼ cup warm water

2 tablespoons extra-virgin olive oil

Juice of 1–2 lemons

2 dashes Worcestershire

2 dashes Tabasco

1 teaspoon salt

To make English muffins: In a bowl combine the powdered milk, 1 tablespoon sugar, ½ teaspoon of the salt, shortening, and hot water. Stir until the sugar and salt are dissolved. Let cool. In a separate bowl, combine the yeast and ⅛ teaspoon sugar in ⅓ cup warm water and let rest until yeast has dissolved. Add this to the dry milk mixture. Add the sifted flour and beat thoroughly with a wooden spoon. Cover the bowl and let rest in a warm spot for 30 minutes.

Preheat a griddle to 300°F.

Add the remaining ½ teaspoon salt to mixture and beat thoroughly. Place 3-inch metal rings onto the griddle and coat lightly with vegetable spray. Using an ice cream scoop, place two scoops (about 3¼ ounces or close to ½ cup) into each ring, then cover the griddle with a pot lid or cookie sheet and cook for 5–6 minutes. Remove the lid and flip the rings using tongs. Again cover with the lid and cook for another 5–6 minutes or until golden brown. Place on a cooling rack, remove rings, and cool.

To prepare hollandaise: Bring about an inch of water to a steady boil in a double boiler. (This allows for a steady and more consistent heat.) You can create a double boiler with a metal bowl that fits into a pot as deep as possible without touching the bottom. Add the egg yolks with the ¼ cup water to the metal bowl and whisk back and forth vigorously over the boiling water. Make sure you are scraping the sides while doing so.

As soon as the yolks start to thicken, turn down the heat and keep whisking until mixture is stiff. Pull off the heat and add the extra-virgin olive oil in a steady slow stream while whisking in circles this time. The olive oil should be warmed beforehand (about 30 seconds in the microwave). Add the rest of the ingredients to taste (the measurements are a good guide).

To assemble sandwich: Cut an English muffin in half. Lay the scrambled eggs on top of the bottom half of the English muffin. Add the bacon and avocado. Top with hollandaise and the top half of the muffin.

Note: Small tuna cans with tops and bottoms removed work well for metal rings.

Mountain Dining

Take a thirty-minute, winding drive up the mountains and you'll find a whole new batch of dining options.

A breakfast/brunch favorite is Silver Fork Lodge, where you can sip coffee and eat sourdough pancakes while listening to the aspen trees whispering all around you.

Dine in a traditional Mongolian yurt at Solitude Mountain Resort and enjoy an exquisite dinner prepared by some of the best chefs in town. Dress appropriately, because you'll be snowshoeing to your dining destination.

Grab a signature Bloody Mary at the St. Regis in Deer Valley. The views from the funicular ride up to the hotel are as grand as the five-star hotel itself.

The Farm at The Canyons provides unforgettable flavors with seasonal and local flare.

Go for a hike or ski day at Sundance Resort and finalize your day with dinner at The Tree Room or a drink from the Owl Bar. Their Sunday brunch at Foundry Grill is also one to enjoy.

Stein Eriksen Lodge boasts years of great food, from their fine dining at the Glitretind, to their brunch buffet with so many options you'll have to come more than once to try all of it.

Seafood is celebrated at Deer Valley's seafood buffet, and wine and small plates shine at The Mariposa. Or, if you really want a treat, take a sleigh ride and enjoy several courses of fondue by the fire at Fireside Dining.

CANNELLA'S

204 EAST 500 SOUTH
SALT LAKE CITY, UTAH 84111
(801) 355-8518
JOEY CANNELLA, OWNER

Salt Lake City is full of neighborhood shops and cafes that locals have walked past for years but perhaps never entered. These places are rooted deep in Utah's restaurant scene, on par with the great staples of great cities that transcend trend and offer a classic taste with a classy room.

Why are they missed? It almost sounds ridiculous to say, but they've been around so long they're almost built into the infrastructure. They're as easy to miss as the temple in downtown Salt Lake City or the mountains to the east. Yes, they're beautiful, but when you see them every day, well, you kind of stop seeing them. After living here for a long time, you miss the obvious things that make this place great. Everyone looks for the newest and latest things, sadly drawing their attention away from the foundation on which the newest and greatest things stand.

Enter Cannella's. In a storied brick building across from Utah's landmark architectural buildings (Salt Lake's city building, city library, public safety building) rests an Italian joint with stories hanging on the walls and family history three generations deep. In many urban areas Cannella's opening year (1978) would almost feel new, but in Utah it's something of a grandfather figure to the growing scene steeped in youth.

Joey and his mom are proud of what has become of the restaurant that the head of the family, Joe Cannella, began years ago. Though it may look and feel different than originally intended, Joey was the perfect match to bring his father's restaurant up to date, offering that same service-forward mentality, with fresh and modern ideas seeping into the menu and atmosphere.

After hearing many people say that the restaurant couldn't survive after the patriarch passed away far too young, Joey felt even more compelled to press onward with the family business. Surviving the recession and his father's passing, Cannella's continues to be a place where friends gather. You might just run into a neighborhood friend at the bar or pull up a chair to an acquaintance on the restaurant side. People who dine here just seem to know each other, or maybe it's the family-like atmosphere that makes people so comfortable that it seems they've known each other for years.

Cannella's may be easy to miss on a busy one-way street, but slow down and stop in and learn a bit more about Utah's culinary past.

Alberto's Meat Lasagna

(SERVES 8–10)

2 yellow bell peppers

2 red bell peppers

1 pound imported lasagna noodles

⅓ pound spicy Italian sausage

⅓ pound ground pork

⅓ pound ground beef

2 pounds ricotta

½ teaspoon dried oregano

½ teaspoon dried parsley

1 tablespoon salt

½ teaspoon pepper

2 pounds mozzarella

¼ cup Parmesan

32 ounces (4 cups) marinara sauce

¼ pound pepperoni

¼ cup Asiago

½ cup balsamic vinegar

2 tablespoons chopped fresh basil

To prepare roasted peppers: Preheat oven to 450°F and line a baking sheet with foil. Place the bell peppers, whole, on the baking sheet and bake for 15 minutes. Flip, then bake another 15 minutes or until the skin on both sides is browned and crisp. Transfer hot peppers to a paper bag to steam. Once cooled, remove the stem and seeds by pulling off the top, then peel off the skins. Transfer the yellow peppers to a blender or food processor and blend until smooth. Repeat with the red peppers. Keep the two pepper purees separate. No seasoning is needed.

To prepare lasagna: Bring a large pot of salted water to a boil. Add lasagna noodles and boil for about 10 minutes.

Meanwhile, in a large pan, cook the sausage. Drain off any excess fat and transfer sausage to a separate plate. In the same pan cook the pork and beef together. Drain and set aside.

In a medium bowl mix the ricotta cheese with oregano, parsley, salt, and pepper. Grate the mozzarella and Parmesan cheese.

Once the noodles are finished cooking al dente (leaving them with a little bite), drain the water from the pan. Preheat oven to 300°F.

Set out all the ingredients to layer for the lasagna in the following five layers:

1. Marinara, noodles, ricotta, mozzarella, beef/pork mixture (use three-quarters)

2. Marinara, noodles, ricotta, mozzarella, pepperoni (use half)

3. Marinara, noodles, ricotta, mozzarella, Parmesan, Asiago

4. Marinara, noodles, ricotta, mozzarella, sausage, beef/pork (use remaining one-quarter)

5. Marinara, noodles, pepperoni (use remaining half), marinara, mozzarella

Place in the oven and bake at 300°F for 45 minutes or, if you're in a hurry, bake at 500°F for 17 minutes. The longer time is preferable.

To prepare the balsamic reduction: While the lasagna is cooking, pour balsamic vinegar into a small pot. Bring to a simmer and reduce by half. This should take 30–45 minutes.

Serving suggestions: Serve the lasagna with a few teaspoonfuls of each bell pepper puree and a drizzle of balsamic reduction over the top. Garnish with fresh basil.

Caputo's on 15th

1516 South 1500 East
Salt Lake City, Utah 84105
(801) 486-6615
CaputosDeli.com
Jamey Chelius, Chef

Caputo's location in the popular 15th and 15th neighborhood offers a little culture of its own in a cross section of town already full of it. Stop in for fine cheese and chocolate, imported oil, or a gourmet Italian sandwich, just as you would at their other much larger flagship shop downtown. But at this location you can also have some hors d'oeuvres and a glass of wine as you sit out on the umbrella-covered patio and watch the neighborhood dogs walk by with their owners.

The smaller shop has its benefits. Get to know the cheesemonger, and make it a habit to visit and sample cheeses regularly. The employees will happily give you recommendations for the best chocolate on their chocolate wall or a new specialty food item worth trying. Caputo's offers many specialty foods that are impossible to find at your average corporate sandwich shop or grocery store—products that the employees are passionate about. Of course they get paid for their work, but the real compensation is working with products and ingredients they believe in. Caputo's on 15th proves that having fewer square feet doesn't detract from the experience. Walk into Jamey's shop, and you'll walk endlessly in circles asking questions about products. Stand in front of the deli case and enjoy conversation and samples for hours. Sip, smell, and taste to a newfound knowledge that could very likely change the way you see food in general.

Stop in for an evening class to learn more about cheese, chocolate, or whiskey. The guys at Caputo's have become something of an authority on these ingredients in recent years.

Those in the 15th and 15th neighborhood know a little secret. Caputo's on 15th serves incredible breakfast sandwiches. Try their Gran Parma Breakfast Sandwich or a feta and tomato panini with mixed greens served on ciabatta. They also serve Charming Beard Coffee, adding to the stack of reasons to come for a relaxed weekend brunch.

Gran Parma Breakfast Sandwich

(SERVES 1)

1 (4-inch) crusty baguette

1 tablespoon unsalted butter, plus extra for baguette

1 thick-cut slice Gran Biscotto ham

1 Clifford Farms egg, cooked over medium

Salt and pepper to taste

1 tablespoon ajvar (roasted red pepper spread found at Middle Eastern markets)

Small handful of arugula

2 slices tomato

1 slice open-eye swiss cheese

Split baguette lengthwise, smear with butter, then place face down in a medium-hot 10-inch sauté pan to toast. Add the tablespoon of butter to a separate pan and fry the egg on medium heat until cooked; salt and pepper to taste. Remove toasted baguette after a minute or two, smear bottom side of bread with ajvar, then layer with arugula, tomato, and egg, and cheese. Top with remaining bread and enjoy.

Tony Caputo's Market and Deli

314 West 300 South
Salt Lake City, Utah 84101
(801) 531-8669
CAPUTOSDELI.COM
Tony and Matt Caputo, Owners

As Salt Lake's major Italian market and deli for over fifteen years, Tony Caputo's is an anchor for local residents. One might even call it a gathering place for those who love food or, better put, "food geeks." Enter their doors and the aroma of fresh meat and aged cheese envelops you. Quickly thereafter, the employees greet you and help you find exactly whatever you're looking for or, even better, something you weren't looking for but now need.

The Caputo's crew loves food, and a cursory conversation with any of them shows it. Perhaps the best part about Caputo's is that they know a little bit about everything and a ton about a few very important things, like cheese and chocolate. Tell them what you're hoping to serve for dinner and they'll get just the right cheese to go along with it. From melt-in-your-mouth French cheese to nutty alpine-style cheeses aged in the Caputo's Cheese Cave, you're sure to find a new favorite. Sample endlessly until you find just the right pairing; when you return on your next visit, your favorite finds are saved in a little note box on their meat and cheese counter.

Matt Caputo, son of Tony, recently became one of the first cheesemongers in the country to sit for the ACS (American Cheese Society) exam and pass. Beyond that, his efforts set the tone for fine chocolate and cheese culture around the city, even putting Utah on the national radar.

The butcher, Frody Volgger, cures and smokes meat with precision and passion. Caputo's offers a robust package of the best possible ingredients from all over the world, including what they call the Local Gold Standard—a group of local producers setting the tone for what best represents local efforts.

Cheese and meat are not the only two fabulous finds at Caputo's; you'll also find the best chocolate selection in the country, ranging from locally made chocolates to international award-winning chocolates (some made locally), and even sparkling chocolate confections from Chocolatier Blue.

Other favorite finds include house-made filled pastas, imported dried pastas, shelves filled with fine oils, vinegars, and gourmet condiments, and the best local products the city has to offer.

THE CAPUTO

(SERVES 1)

1 crusty peasant bread roll, 6–8 inches in length, sliced through the middle
1 ounce extra-virgin olive oil
1 ounce quality balsamic vinegar
1½ ounces sliced mortadella
1½ ounces thinly sliced Genoa salami
1 ounce sliced prosciutto
1½ ounces sliced provolone cheese
4 slices tomato
Lettuce leaves
Sicilian marinated olives and pepperoncini

Place the bread on a cutting board and drizzle one half with the olive oil and the other half with the balsamic vinegar, covering the entire surface of the bread. Fold the mortadella in half and distribute evenly on the bottom half of the roll. Add the Genoa salami and prosciutto followed by the provolone cheese. Top with sliced tomatoes and lettuce leaves, cover with the top half of the bread, and slice the sandwich in half. Garnish with Sicilian marinated olives and pepperoncini.

CHAIA CUCINA

(385) 212-4242
CHAIACUCINA.COM
ADAM KREISEL, CHEF/OWNER

Restaurants can't contain Adam Kreisel, and kitchens can't get rid of him. He's a one-of-a-kind, Boston-born, skiing hippy of sorts, who abandoned the life of owning his own restaurants or executive chef roles at other restaurants for the glories of catering. He makes his own schedule this way. Catering gives him the freedom to go to mecca once a year (Fenway Park) with the great light in his life, his daughter, Chaia. He feels that he maintains sanity with a constantly changing menu not found in the overwhelming day-to-day restaurant life.

Chaia translates from Hebrew to English as "life giving," which seems to be Adam's approach to cooking, parenthood, and just about everything else. Adam loves (and executes well) a perfect soup made with the right seasonal ingredients. He geeks out on complicated yet accessible dishes. But he lights up the most when asked about his daughter. A rich relationship with her shines through in his creative cooking. If you're really lucky, when you hire Chaia Cucina for your private event, he'll bring Chaia along to cheer up the service crew in the kitchen and keep a smile on the chef's face.

When not meeting with clients or spending time prepping for private events, Adam is busy with S.L.U.R.P. For the uninitiated out there, this stands for Soup Lends Understanding, Relaxation and Pleasure. It's a soup club started by Adam for his fans who were disappointed that they didn't have regular access to his menu at restaurants anymore. Once a month he fashions a soup creation, goes to a neutral location known by S.L.U.R.P. advocates, and sells it.

In knowing Adam a few years, we've learned that he is always up to something else. He alludes to something meaningful on the horizon but won't volunteer the concept. In due time, I suppose. No doubt it will be worth supporting and tasting.

LIGHTLY SPICED ROASTED CAULIFLOWER AND PEAR BISQUE

(SERVES 12)

1 large head cauliflower

1 tablespoon pure/pomace olive oil

½ teaspoon salt

1 medium parsnip, peeled

1 teaspoon pure/pomace olive oil

⅛ teaspoon salt

½ cup pure/pomace olive oil

3 cloves garlic, sliced thin

2½ tablespoons (about 1 ounce) roughly chopped fresh
    ginger

1–1½ cups finely diced sweet onion

1 tablespoon prepared Thai green curry paste

1 cup (2–3 stalks) finely diced celery

1 cup white wine

2 quarts vegetable stock

2 cups peeled and diced Yukon Gold potatoes

1 cup heavy cream

1½ fresh pears (about 2 cups) (Anjou work well),
    skin-on, cut medium dice, cores discarded

1 tablespoon roughly chopped fresh thyme leaves

1 tablespoon whole fennel seed

½ cup agave syrup or local honey

Lemon juice, as needed

Kosher salt and ground black Telicherry peppercorns

Preheat oven to 350°F. Dice the cauliflower and toss with 1 tablespoon olive oil and ½ teaspoon salt. Dice the parsnip and toss with 1 teaspoon olive oil and ⅛ teaspoon salt. Place cauliflower and parsnip onto separate pans. Roast the cauliflower for about 45 minutes and the parsnip for about 20 minutes, until both are sweet, slightly softened, and starting to caramelize on the outside. Remove from the oven and reserve.

In a large soup or stockpot set on medium-high heat, add the ½ cup olive oil, garlic, ginger, sweet onion, and green curry paste and sweat until translucent and just starting to caramelize. Add the roasted cauliflower, roasted parsnips, celery, and white wine and stir to combine. Add the vegetable stock and potatoes and allow the pot to come to a simmer. Stir in the heavy cream, pears, thyme, and fennel seed. Allow the soup to lightly simmer until all the veggies and potatoes are nicely softened. Turn off the heat and add the agave syrup, a squeeze or two of lemon juice, and several good pinches of salt and pepper.

Working in batches, puree the soup in a Vitamixer or other excellent high-speed blender. The final texture of the soup is a matter of personal preference. If you prefer the soup to have a lighter, smoother, velvety texture, you may need to taste it repeatedly as you are blending. If you feel that the soup is too thick, you can drizzle in small amounts of cold water as the batches of soup are blending, to achieve your desired texture. Transfer each batch of blended soup into a vessel large enough to hold all of the finished product.

Taste the soup and adjust the seasoning as desired with small additions of agave syrup, lemon juice, salt, or pepper. Ideally, the flavor of the soup should be round and savory with a touch of sweetness and a bit of heat at the finish from the curry paste. Typically, your palate will recognize the cauliflower first, then the fruitiness of the pear, and finish with the mild bite of the curry.

CHANON THAI

278 East 900 South
Salt Lake City, Utah 84102
(801) 532-1177
CHANONTHAI.COM
Sasipa Chanon, Owner

What qualities should one look for in a Thai restaurant? Besides the food, of course, it needs to be a little quirky with authentic regional knickknacks as decor, intriguing translations on the menus, handwritten signs, mix-matched Corelle dishes, hand-drawn menus, and waiters whose first language is, well, Thai. At Chanon Thai, the "Open" sign out front is sometimes flickering, a few letters might be missing light, and you never know if the front door will be open even if all the letters stand proudly lit. If they are open, the dining room is usually packed. All this makes Chanon Thai a gold mine for those wanting an experience rooted in great food and not one hidden in overelaborate decor or distracting ambience.

Anyone hunting for a traditional Thai experience in Salt Lake finds it in the food and service at Chanon. This small, charming restaurant is owned and run by one woman, her two daughters, and their husbands. The daughters share managerial roles while mom enjoys the kitchen, cooking the same traditional dishes she created during her twenty years of cooking in Thailand. The family behind Chanon Thai prides themselves in taking a role to educate locals on Thai dining culture. When ordering, keep in mind that traditional dishes are shared, not served for individual consumption as western

convention prescribes. Should you be set on ordering the old-fashioned American way, your server readily informs you that Thai food is communal, not individual.

On a menu full of authentic treasure, the Gang Dang (red curry) dominates in our opinion. I'm sure plenty of other dishes warrant ordering, like the Kaow Pad Sub Pa Rod (pineapple cashew fried rice) or the tender calamari and the larb salad. But one taste of the Gang Dang, and our cravings find satisfaction only in its spicy, creamy delight.

The Gang Dang submerges vegetables like bamboo shoots, eggplant, zucchini, and buttercup squash in a creamy coconut curry sauce with your choice of meat or tofu. Chanon offers a scale of one to ten for spiciness. Choose wisely and avoid attempts at proving your arrogant spice capacity. Thai spice never awards the brave; it only punishes.

GANG DANG CURRY

(SERVES 4)

3 cups coconut milk

2 tablespoons red curry paste

1 cup uncooked protein (chicken, beef, or tofu), sliced
    into bite-sized pieces

1 teaspoon chicken bouillon powder

½ cup vegetable stock

1½ tablespoons fish sauce

1½ tablespoons sugar

1 Kaffir lime leaf, torn in half

1 cup mixed vegetables (Chanon uses red and green
    bell pepper, buttercup squash, zucchini, eggplant,
    and bamboo shoot slices)

2–3 Thai basil leaves, plus more for garnish

Bring coconut milk to a boil in a large pot. Add curry paste and let melt into the coconut milk. Add protein and all spices from bouillon to Kaffir lime leaf. Don't stir. Cook until coconut milk starts to boil again, then stir.

When protein is almost done cooking (3–5 minutes), add in raw vegetables. Bring to a boil again. Tear the Thai basil and stir into the pot. Taste and add more spice, salt, and sugar to your liking. Cook 1 more minute, then serve over rice.

Garnish with additional Thai basil.

Chow Truck

INFO@CHOWTRUCK.COM
SuAn Chow, Chef/Owner

When you think of food trucks in Salt Lake City, your first thought is likely Chow Truck. The big yellow machine moved its way through the streets of Salt Lake as the first food truck of consequence in the city.

SuAn Chow paved the way for local food trucks to hit the streets in Salt Lake, but the path was by no means easy. She fought the city for this unique dining experience for months. Now many food trucks enjoy the freedoms of serving Salt Lake residents without a brick and mortar, and didn't have to cut through the red tape.

Chow Truck brings healthier fast food to residents all over the valley. Her success hinges on it. The menu is simple, which in her opinion is the best kind of menu. Haute Asian cuisine dialed and perfected, served fast and fresh, is the specialty of her rolling restaurant. Behind the glass window and ice buffet of drink choices, the service system is quick and efficient. Long waits are not part of the experience, only tasty food.

Pick a protein, like the coconut-lemon grass chicken or panko-dusted tofu, then select either a taco, slider, or salad to pair. The Asian Spiced Root Chips are the perfect side: crispy, colorful, beautiful vegetables with a spice you can't quite put your finger on but can't take your hands off.

SuAn Chow opened the market for food trucks in SLC, and now the streets rejoice.

ASIAN SPICED ROOT CHIPS

(SERVES 10)

For the root vegetables:

2 medium-sized yams

2 medium-sized Yukon Gold potatoes

2 medium-sized purple potatoes

2 medium-sized red beets

1 medium-sized lotus root

Canola or soy oil, for frying

For the seasoned salt:

2 tablespoons kosher salt

2 teaspoons white pepper

2 teaspoons Chinese five-spice powder

To prepare the root chips: Thinly slice each root vegetable with a mandoline, then deep fry one root vegetable at a time in canola or soy oil at 220°F until crisp. Remove and drain excess oil on paper towels.

To prepare the seasoned salt: Stir salt, pepper, and five-spice powder until well combined. Shake the seasoned salt on chips while hot.

FOOD CARTS

While tacos carts have been on the scene in Utah for quite some time, the more modern food cart trend hit the city only recently. The Chow Truck, serving haute Asian cuisine such as tacos, sliders, and salads, was the first to pave the way. While the trucks jaunt around the city throughout the week, you can count on a small gathering of food carts convening at the Gallivan Center every Thursday during lunchtime. Here are a few food trucks to keep an eye out for:

Submarinos: serves sandwiches and soup made with from-scratch ingredients.

Off the Grid: serves waffles topped with untraditional ingredients like slow-roasted pork, local Beehive cheddar cheese, or spicy grilled chicken.

Gravy Train: provides a taste of the French Canadian classic, *poutine*: a generous helping of french fries, cheese curds, and gravy.

Cup Bop: serves Korean barbecue in a takeaway cup with your choice of meat, veggies, and rice or noodles.

A Guy and His Wife Grilled Cheese: offers gourmet grilled cheese sandwiches with fresh-cut curly fries.

Saturday's Waffle: features an Airstream trailer serving up gourmet Liège waffles.

Lewis Brothers: serves up unique burgers with flavorful additions like kimchi, as well as *banh mi* sandwiches.

Waki Paki: gives a taste of Pakistani street food.

Better Burger: features grass-fed beef burgers, turkey burgers, and one-of-a-kind veggie burgers.

Church and State Spirits

(801) 463-1503

Sean Neves, Scott Gardner, Matt Pfohl, Bartenders

Three guys lead the way in Utah's sea change of spirits. Matt Pfohl, Scott Gardner, and Sean Neves all ran incredibly successful bar programs at some of Utah's more reputable restaurants before inching toward the cliff that Holden Caulfield warned his sister about leading into the world of owning their own operation.

Three successful bartenders in the Salt Lake community can't all come together under one roof and behind one bar, can they? Can three egos coexist and run smoothly? The absence of ego is precisely why Sean, Matt, and Scott work so well together. Ego generally comes in the absence of skill. When skill can't speak for itself, egos grow as compensation for what is lacking on the plate or in the glass. These guys let the cocktails speak. There's no false humility here. They know they're good, otherwise they wouldn't be cashing it all in to start their own spot. Approach a bar tended by any of these three, and you'll quickly see that pretense isn't their game. They realize that ego distances the barman from his people. These guys are for the people.

Think of them as doctors. Yes, they're all in the same category, bartender, but look closer. They're specialists, like a neurologist or a cardiovascular surgeon. On the surface the cocktail virgin might accuse them of being the same, but look deeper, and three highly specialized professionals emerge.

Scott Gardner makes cocktails like Brittanica makes encyclopedias. From beginning to end, Scott can tell you the history of every liquor in the glass and the philosophy behind its production. Matt Pfohl is something of a love doctor. Every cocktail speaks beautiful poetry. Take one drink and you really don't care what's in it. You're mesmerized by its passion and perfect fit for the day's mood. Sean Neves embodies Utah. He knows

its history, loves the Jazz, and pushes hard to see it all elevate. He's the business mind of the three, who makes a cocktail with a nod to Utah's past and an abundance of love and passion for what's in the glass and the person drinking it.

The state of spirits in Utah is safe thanks to these guys and about a dozen other bartenders who are changing Utah's horizon.

CHURCH & STATE PUNCH

BY SCOTT GARDNER

(SERVES 1)

1 ounce Jamaican rum (we use Smith & Cross)
¾ ounce VSOP cognac (we use Gautier)
½ ounce Oloroso sherry (we use Bodegas Hidalgo)
½ ounce fresh lemon juice
½ ounce black tea syrup
1 dash angostura bitters
Lemon peel
Nutmeg, whole

Add all ingredients to a shaker. Shake vigorously for 20–25 seconds. Twist lemon peel into a chilled cocktail glass, so the lemon oil coats the glass. Strain punch into the glass over a small "block" of clear ice. Grate fresh nutmeg over the surface of the punch.

Jaibica

BY MATT PFOHL

(SERVES 1)

1½ ounces bacanora (use blanco mezcal if bacanora is unavailable)

¾ ounce dolin blanc (can use a dry vermouth if blanc styles are unavailable)

½ ounce grappa

¼ ounce luxardo maraschino

1 dash orange bitters

Lemon peel

Add all ingredients to a mixing glass. Fill the glass with ice to three-quarters full. Stir the drink for about 20–25 seconds. Strain into a chilled cocktail glass. Twist lemon peel over the surface of the drink and garnish with the peel.

Note: *Jaibica* is the small ax used to harvest the agave in traditional bacanora production.

COMMUNAL

102 NORTH UNIVERSITY AVENUE
PROVO, UTAH 84601
(801) 373-8000
COMMUNALRESTAURANT.COM
COLTON SOELBERG AND JOSEPH MCRAE, OWNERS
JOHN NEWMAN, CHEF DE CUISINE

If you need more proof of the elevating restaurant scene in Utah, spend a few evenings dining out in Provo. Provo gets a bad rap for being homogeneous and stereotyped as a sort of suburbia haven. Yes, there are large families in Utah County who, out of necessity, are looking for inexpensive meals to feed large families. At the same time, a constituency of folks are looking for something better, something that justifies a night out on the town but doesn't take the forty-five-minute drive from Provo to Salt Lake.

The Heirloom Restaurant Group saw those interested in something different/ better and created Communal. Though not their first attempt in Utah (Pizzeria 712 being their first), Communal certainly made a strong statement, which resonated up to the neighborhoods of downtown Salt Lake.

In an area where faster and cheaper is most valued, Communal provides an evening out on the town at your choice of communal or private tables with a menu filled with fresh, seasonal ingredients and a chef sure to satisfy the most cosmopolitan of tastes in great slow-food fashion.

The concept is in the name—literally from farm to table. Long communal tables cutting through the center of the room tell a story of Communal's philosophy of relationships with farmers, local producers, and customers. It begs strangers to say hello, creating a relationship where there might not have been one before. Even if the common topics of the valley don't strike your fancy, the food is worth talking about.

A night at the table generally finds diners getting to know each other, learning about local farms, and tasting through a menu that makes a statement that Provo is worth it. While it does save locals the long drive to Salt Lake City, the Salt Lake foodies are driving farther than they ever thought they would for something better than they could ever have imagined.

COMMUNAL BEET SALAD

(SERVES 6–8)

For the pistachio brittle:

2 cups granulated sugar
1 cup water
½ cup corn syrup
½ teaspoon kosher salt
2 tablespoons butter
½ teaspoon baking soda
2½ cups chopped pistachios
2 tablespoons chopped dill

For the pistachio dill pesto:

¼ cup fresh dill
¼ cup raw, shelled pistachios
½ cup spinach
Juice of 1 lemon
Salt and pepper

For the roasted beets:

½ pound red or yellow beets
2 tablespoons extra-virgin olive oil
Salt and pepper
Zest of 2 lemons

For garnish:

Shaved radishes and fennel
Arugula
Goat cheese
Extra-virgin olive oil

To prepare pistachio brittle: In a heavy saucepan over medium heat, bring sugar, water, corn syrup, and salt to a caramel color without burning. Remove from heat and add butter, baking soda, chopped pistachios, and dill. Mix together and pour caramel onto a parchment-lined (also coat parchment with nonstick vegetable spray) sheet pan and let cool.

To prepare pistachio dill pesto: Place all ingredients in a blender and puree until smooth. If too thick, add cold water. Season with salt and pepper.

To prepare roasted beets: Preheat oven to 250°F. Season beets with oil, salt, and pepper. Wrap in foil and roast for 2–3 hours or until soft and tender. Allow to cool and peel outer skin. Toss with lemon zest.

To serve: Arrange pesto on a plate. Plate beets and serve with pistachio brittle, shaved radish, shaved fennel, arugula, goat cheese, and olive oil.

Skirt Steak and Chermoula

(SERVES 6)

For the chermoula:

2 bunches parsley

1 bunch cilantro

3 cloves garlic

1 teaspoon cumin

2 teaspoons paprika

¼ teaspoon chili flakes

Juice of 2 lemons

½ cup blended oil

¼ cup white wine vinegar

Olive oil

1 (1½ pounds) skirt steak

Coarse salt and pepper

To prepare chermoula: Puree all ingredients in a blender.

To prepare skirt steak: Preheat grill on high. While grill is heating, allow steak to come to room temperature. This will ensure even cooking.

Lightly oil and season steak with coarse salt and pepper. Place steak on grill and cook on both sides until desired temperature is reached. Remove steak from grill and allow to rest for 3–5 minutes. Slice and serve with the chermoula.

Copper Onion

111 East Broadway
Salt Lake City, Utah 84111
(801) 355-3282
THECOPPERONION.COM
Ryan Lowder, Chef/Owner

Every city in America claims a restaurant whose lore and legend exceed the hopes of the most ambitious of restaurateurs. Copper Onion is Salt Lake City's urban treasure. Perhaps the restaurant's greatest accomplishment surpasses simply filling the seats day after day and night after night. Many restaurants boast waiting lists and great reviews online. Copper Onion's greatest achievement can be summarized in one simple dish: bone marrow.

Salt Lake City diners now eat bone marrow.

How did that happen? Through vision, brilliance, a great staff, and happenstance. The Copper Onion's earlier days comprised more traditional items, though still compelling. By doing the more accessible things really well (hamburgers and such), chef/owner Ryan Lowder developed a fan base that trusts the menu.

Trust is Copper Onion's most valuable currency, and Lowder has wisely spent time slowly turning up the volume on Utah's burgeoning palate.

And now? Now Utahans are willing to try things they've never tried before. And they like it.

Darken Copper Onion's doors, and you'll likely meet a boisterous wine enthusiast named Jimmy Santangelo. He's a tall distance runner with a Jersey accent who knows his way around the wine store. One of a handful of sommeliers in town, Santangelo's wine list is sure to satisfy the range of tastes coming in and out of Copper Onion. As is par for the sommelier course, Jimmy also dabbles in cocktails, and he has settled in nicely to Salt Lake City's emerging cocktail scene.

Utahans interested in moving beyond the typical local fare are proud of Copper Onion. Trust its menu; it will take you somewhere you never thought you'd go.

BEEF STROGANOFF

(SERVES 4 AS A MAIN COURSE)

For the beef:

1 pound chuck tail or chuck roast, cut into chunks

1 cup chopped onion

1 cup sliced celery

1 cup sliced carrot

4 cloves garlic

2 bay leaves

2 sprigs thyme

Water or stock

For the stroganoff:

1 pound cremini mushrooms, sliced

2 tablespoons extra-virgin olive oil

2 tablespoons butter

1 small shallot, sliced

2 cloves garlic, sliced

½ cup heavy cream

1 cup braising liquid

Salt and pepper to taste

8 ounces pappardelle pasta

½ cup crème fraîche

¼ cup fresh chives

To prepare the beef: Brown the meat in a nonstick pan over high heat. Do not overcrowd pan; brown in batches if needed. Place the beef, onions, celery, carrots, garlic, bay leaves, and thyme in an oven-safe dish. Add enough water or stock to cover. Cover dish and cook in a 325°F oven for 3–5 hours. Check after a few hours and add more water or stock if necessary to keep meat and vegetables covered.

When meat is fork tender, remove it from the oven. Set the meat aside to cool and strain the liquid from the vegetables. Discard veggies. Cool liquid and skim most of the fat from the top. Reserve this braising liquid for later.

To prepare the stroganoff: Toss mushrooms with olive oil and a sprinkling of salt. Roast in a 375°F oven for 15–20 minutes.

In a sauté pan over medium heat, melt the butter, then add the shallot, garlic, and roasted mushrooms and cook until tender, about 5 minutes. Add the beef, cream, and reserved braising liquid and cook until liquid is reduced and thickened, about 7 minutes. Add salt and pepper to taste.

Meanwhile, bring a large pot of salted water to a boil over high heat. Add the pasta and cook until al dente. Drain the pasta, then add it to the sauté pan and cook for 2 minutes.

Serve stroganoff immediately with a dollop of crème fraîche and fresh chives.

One estate winery exists in Utah. *One.* One could easily conclude that the land in Utah can't sustain a thriving vineyard churning out great fruit year after year, and that's why only one estate stands on Utah soil. But it's not the soil's fault. Many experts conclude that the soil profiles are quite conducive to growing riesling, blaufrankisch, gruner veltliner, kerner, and other lesser-known varietals. If not the land, then what? It's easy to swing to the opposite end of the pendulum and blame the government for its restrictions and obstacles for aspiring Utah viticulturists. That's not it either. As is typical, the answer isn't found in the extremes, it's found in the balance.

Simply put, Utah is a burgeoning scene on every level, including wine. At the forefront of the forward charge stand two guys trumpeting a call to the locals to come taste the compelling fruit of the vine. But don't stop at a taste. Understand it. Make a relationship with it. See that the metaphysical miracle in the glass warrants more than just a passive taste. Understanding wine opens the drinker up to other cultures, other soils, and other values worth exploring.

Locals know the men and their cause well: Evan Lewandowski of Ruth Lewandowski Wines and sommelier at Pago, and Jimmy Santangelo, sommelier at the Copper Onion and owner of the Utah Wine Academy. Each one tells a different story about wine, with dozens of converts to the slippery and pricey slope of wine affection.

JIMMY SANTANGELO

Spend an evening at a table at the Copper Onion when Jimmy works the floor, and you'll feel like you have a new best friend. He exudes a professionalism and casualness sure to satisfy the elitist wine snob and the average Joe who refers to wine solely as red or white, never mind the pink stuff. He reads his customers well and gauges their wine knowledge quickly, but he doesn't judge them, even when it would be really easy and embarrassingly fun to do so.

This quality of embracing the person for where they're at while pushing them deeper into wine culture summarizes Jimmy best. His Wine Academy of Utah exists to do just that: teach people about elements of wine previously unknown. Sitting in Jimmy's classroom, you'll find University of Utah Lifelong Learning Program students learning just for fun as well as career servers looking for more knowledge and understanding to better help them serve their wine list (most likely put together or influenced by Jimmy).

Perhaps the greatest and most interesting feather in Jimmy's cap is his classes that teach non-alcohol-drinking servers how to sell a wine tableside. He doesn't pretend he's not in Utah. That's a very real challenge here. Many servers observe a faith that doesn't allow even a taste of an item they're supposed to be able to sell. Rather than ignore the challenge, Jimmy came up with a class based on sight and smell, bringing fresh fruits of varying color and ripeness to aid in his explanation of the varying varietals of wine.

Much of the wine scene is in debt to Jimmy's work behind the pulpit teaching the depth and complexity and beauty of wine. Without him Utah most certainly would still drink wine, but likely know less about it.

EVAN LEWANDOWSKI

Take a look at Jimmy's wine list and compare it to Evan's list at Pago. Jimmy's is like the Rolling Stones, and Evan's is like that obscure band that you've never heard but after one listen you're in love. Evan digs and finds winemakers and vintages from operations yielding small batches of complex, mostly atypical wines. No big, oaky cabs on his menu, though they can be crowd pleasers. Evan's taste and understanding of pairing won't let him phone it in with something that doesn't do the greatest justice to the fruit in the vineyard and the land from which it comes.

Beyond developing Pago's wine list and moving from table to table charming the diners, Evan makes wine. He spent years developing his love for wine and the art of making it in Alsace, Alto Adige, Tuscany, Argentina, California, New Zealand, and Australia to prepare for his return to make wine in Utah. His first vintage, 2012, came and went long before the 2013s released with great fanfare in Paris, New York, San Francisco, and most important, Utah.

If it isn't already obvious, Evan's winemaking is different than that of the average winemaker. He works in small batches and largely takes a laissez-faire approach to his wines. Don't take that the wrong way. Though he fights tooth and nail to abstain from additives of any style, he monitors fermentation and aging closely. He's no stranger to the microscope and spends hours geeking out on numbers and measurements hardly understood by the outside world. He believes the best way he can do justice to the fruit and the processes it naturally goes through is to do everything possible to ensure you only taste what naturally occurs.

The future of wine rests in able hands. Jimmy and Evan are only two of the sommeliers and wine brokers and wine drinkers elevating the wine scene in Utah. Of course, the job of establishing, sustaining, and elevating a wine program in Utah takes more than just two handsome guys. There are several folks in the industry also worth mentioning for their contribution.

Francis Fecteau operates Libation, a local wine broker responsible for many wines in the liquor stores and in restaurants. Louis Koppel from By the Glass, formerly of Spencer's Steak and Chops, is a sommelier's sommelier working the floor and moving wines with great passion and love. Finally, no story of wine is complete without Cara Schwindt. Her wine cellar runs deep at the Stein Eriksen Lodge in Deer Valley, boasting one of the most robust lists in the state.

Wine in Utah offers a snapshot of the cliché that it takes a village. No one person or entity could change the tide of a state on its own.

CREMINELLI FINE MEATS

310 North Wright Brothers Drive
Salt Lake City, Utah 84116
(801) 428-1820
CREMINELLI.COM
Cristiano Creminelli, Owner/Maker

Cristiano Creminelli talks about salami like a mother talks about her child. Creating salami of this caliber requires parent-like attention with a long, careful commitment to moving it from infancy to maturity. Fine meats and cheeses are certainly all the rage in Utah, thanks to the likes of Tony Caputo's Market and Deli and Liberty Heights Fresh's eye-opening selections and customer service, but don't accuse Cristiano of chasing the latest trend. He's a fourteenth-generation maker of fine meats from northern Italy who found Utah in a pursuit comparable to an uncompromising story of love.

Where some companies might use terms like "handcrafted" or "artisanal," Creminelli Fine Meats wrote the book on it. Cristiano is known to take multiple trips a day to his

warehouse to simply smell and feel every piece of salami aging in a maze of rooms. From beginning to end, Cristiano's approach to salami displays respect for a craft and a philosophy long since forgotten in a world generally more concerned with speed over quality and quantity over virtue.

When Cristiano arrived in Salt Lake City in 2006, he started production in the basement of Tony Caputo's Market and Deli, where he obsessed over salami and quickly outgrew the basement in stature, production, and offerings. He stayed in the realm of fine meats, but took his skill and meticulous attention to detail and produced a series of world-class fine deli meats—Mortadella (emulsified blend of pork and spices) and Prosciutto Cotto (a flakier, spicier, more aromatic version of American ham), to name a couple.

Cristiano's descent on Utah runs parallel with the time when Utahans began to see local producers as agents of change. Creminelli led locals to love salami. And if salami can be this good, what else? Cheese? Coffee? Wine? Though the local producers may not use Cristiano's name as the sole inspiration of their business, many would note that he paved the way and proved the concept that good business is more than just cheap ingredients, higher margins, and faster production. Good business is about a damn good product.

Salami Milano Involtini

(SERVES 4)

1 sheet puff pastry, thawed (follow thawing instructions
   on package)

9–10 slices salami milano (sliced about the width of a
   dime)

9–10 slices provolone cheese

¼ cup milk

Preheat oven to 400°F.

Spread pastry on a lightly floured flat surface.
Cover pastry with milano slices, then place
provolone slices on top of salami. Roll up pastry
dough, jelly-roll style, pinching the ends to make
sure that the cheese and salami do not slip out.
When finished rolling, seal the end of the dough
against itself.

Using a knife, cut the roll into slices approximately
1 inch wide. Place slices face up on a baking
sheet lined with parchment paper. Be sure slices
are far enough apart that the puff pastry has
room to puff out while baking. Brush tops of
slices with milk.

Bake for 15–20 minutes, until the cheese on top
is browned and slightly crispy. Note that smaller
slices will bake faster than larger slices and may
need to be removed from the oven earlier.

Allow to cool for 5 minutes before serving. Serve
warm.

Deer Valley Grocery Cafe

1375 Deer Valley Drive
Park City, Utah 84060
(435) 615-2400
DEERVALLEY.COM
Jodie Rogers, Executive Chef

Generally when you think of ski food, overpriced burgers and heartburn-inducing chili may be the first things that come to mind. Deer Valley unreservedly redefines ski resort food, bringing in some of the best chefs from around the world to feed hungry skiers well beyond their imaginations.

Deer Valley lies less than an hour's drive from Salt Lake and provides well-groomed slopes in view of opulent hotels and private ski homes. But you don't have to be made of money to feel grand skiing Deer Valley. Locals make their way to this Park City resort for some of the best skiing in the state married with the best ski foods you can fit on a wobbly tray while wearing awkward ski boots.

Trade a dried-out burger for a house-made bratwurst cooked just the way you like it with all the trimmings. The famous Deer Valley turkey chili station may have a line, but once you have a few bites, the hype justifies the line. The Carvery features two roasts daily served with gourmet sauces like béchamel or fresh thyme and lemon. It's not often you combine skiing with a New York strip and one of the mother sauces. For those looking for lighter fare, the Natural Buffet is a round of endless vegetable choices, grains, legumes, fish, and greens. Go ahead and splurge on the larger salad plate.

And since you have been hitting the slopes hard all morning, you may as well hit the baked goods too. Jumbo cookies, brownies, and fresh-made desserts like the Deep Powder Carrot Cake give that extra boost of sugar to motivate a few more turns on the mountain.

While Utah boasts of a host of amazing ski resorts from which to choose, if you like a superior meal to go along with great powder, Deer Valley delivers. *Ski Magazine* readers repeatedly give Deer Valley top rankings in on-mountain food. Go see why.

ROASTED BUTTERNUT SQUASH
AND ANASAZI BEAN ENCHILADAS

(SERVES 8)

For the enchiladas:

3 cups roasted, diced butternut squash

2 cups cooked Anasazi beans

1 cup julienned shiitake mushrooms, sautéed in 2
    tablespoons olive oil

1 cup roasted corn

¼ cup roasted pumpkin seeds

1 cup chopped cilantro

Salt and pepper to taste

8 (8-inch) white corn tortillas

1 cup grated cheddar cheese

1 cup grated jack cheese

½ cup cilantro sour cream (see below)

For the cilantro sour cream, stir together:

½ bunch cilantro, washed and chopped

1 lime, zested and juiced

1¼ teaspoons pureed garlic

14 ounces sour cream

1 teaspoon salt

¼ teaspoon black pepper

For the roasted tomatillo cilantro sauce:

6 pounds, 10 ounces tomatillos, peeled and roasted

4 bunches cilantro, washed

⅓ cup pureed garlic

¾ cup plus 4 teaspoons chopped shallots

3 pounds, 5 ounces Anaheim chile peppers, roasted,
    seeded, and peeled

3 pounds, 5 ounces poblano peppers, roasted, seeded,
    and peeled

8 teaspoons salt

4 cups water

1¼ cups (2½ sticks) butter, room temperature, cut into
    ½-inch pieces

To prepare the enchiladas: Preheat oven to
350°F. Mix the squash, beans, mushrooms, corn,
pumpkin seeds, cilantro, and salt and pepper
together, being careful not to overmix into a
puree.

Top each tortilla with approximately 1 cup
enchilada mix, some of both cheeses, and a
dollop of cilantro sour cream.

Roll filled tortillas and place into a baking pan.
Cover and bake for 20 minutes.

Remove from oven and top with the roasted
tomatillo cilantro sauce and remaining cheeses.
Return to oven to melt cheese over the top of the
enchiladas.

Use remaining sour cream as a garnish over top
of the heated enchiladas.

To prepare the cilantro sour cream: Combine
all ingredients in a mixing bowl and blend
thoroughly.

To prepare the roasted tomatillo cilantro sauce: In
a food processor or blender, puree all ingredients
except butter. Transfer to a large sauté pan and
bring to a boil. Turn down heat and simmer for
20–30 minutes, stirring constantly. Turn off heat
and add the pieces of cold butter to the sauce.
Chill.

Sauce may be kept refrigerated for up to 5 days.
Add water for proper consistency if reheating
becomes necessary.

DOTTIE'S BISCUIT BARN

facebook.com/dottiesbiscuitbarn
ANDY WALTER, OWNER

You haven't lived until you've seen a biscuit barn drive down the busy streets of Salt Lake City only to stop near you, open the barn doors, and benevolently pour gravy on perfect biscuits and place them in your hands. A fairer person you'll never meet, Andy Walter slaves overnight to prepare the awe-inspiring fare of Dottie's Biscuit Barn before every Downtown Farmers Market he graces. True to Utah's generous style, other restaurant owners with commercial kitchens open their doors for Andy to come in during their restaurants' dormant hours in the middle of the night to make biscuits, gravy, and pie.

If you see Andy at the Downtown Farmers Market, you'll notice he looks pretty tired. He doesn't look that way because he woke up early. The bags under his eyes prove that he actually hasn't been to sleep yet. Locals know his smiling face from his time serving customers at the Copper Onion or managing the Shallow Shaft up near Alta. An average Friday evening finds Andy working his day job, clocking out, then heading to a kitchen to cook until the early risers of the farmers' market heed the call of biscuits.

Perhaps a brick and mortar is in the future, but for now Andy can't make enough biscuits for the markets he attends or the parties he caters. The barn is always the hype of the markets and the joy of the lucky ones who taste the wonders of Dottie's biscuits.

If you ever see a barn driving down the street, follow it. For one, it's probably not going far because gas prices are high. And two, biscuits, gravy, and Andy's friendly face await.

TOMATO GRAVY

(SERVES 4–6)

3–4 (about 2½ pounds) large, ripe heirloom tomatoes
½ large yellow onion
1 Anaheim or similarly mild to medium-heat pepper
1 sweet pepper (use yellow and green to add color, or whatever is coming in from the garden)
½ jalapeño or more intense pepper (serrano or cayenne could work too)
1 tablespoon butter
½ tablespoon salt
¾ teaspoon cracked pepper
½ tablespoon smoked paprika
½ tablespoon fresh oregano
½ teaspoon red pepper flakes (depending on what peppers you used in the sauté)
2 cups vegetable stock

For the roux:

4 tablespoons butter or lard
¼ cup flour
Salt and pepper to taste

Prepare a large saucepan with boiling water, then cut a small *X* in the bottom of each tomato and drop them in for a couple of minutes. Remove to an ice bath and peel the skins after a minute or two in the ice water. Once peeled, take the firmest tomatoes and dice them up. The softer ones (depends on varietal and ripeness), cut up as best as possible, or just crush by hand and save for adding to the sauté.

Medium dice the onion and peppers.

Put 1 tablespoon butter or other cooking fat (bacon lard would work great too!) into a large sauté pan and add onions and peppers. Sauté until onions are translucent and begin to caramelize . . . the more color the better!

Add the salt, pepper, smoked paprika, oregano, and red pepper flakes, give the mixture a quick stir, and then add half the tomatoes (using the crushed and/or roughly cut tomatoes first). Let the tomato juice deglaze the pan (you could use a touch of red wine at this point as well). Once the tomatoes are hot, add in the vegetable stock and allow the sauce to come up to a boil, then reduce heat slightly and allow the sauce to gently boil for half an hour. Give the sauce time to reduce down a touch and naturally thicken.

Adjust your spices as needed during this time. At the end of this reduction, add the other half of the diced tomatoes (not including their juices). This will preserve the "chunk" of the tomato gravy.

To prepare the roux: Melt the butter or lard and then stir in the flour in batches, using a whisk and stirring vigorously. The longer you "cook" the roux, the less thickening properties (starchiness) it will have in your sauce. The French have all sorts of classifications for these cook times; however, the longer you cook the roux, the more flavors will emerge. Once the flour is incorporated, I cook the roux for about 2–3 minutes on medium heat, constantly stirring. Save the roux; it keeps for a long time.

Note: This is a butter and flour roux, but if you want to make it gluten free you could use a cornstarch slurry, tapioca flour, etc.

Slowly add ½ cup roux to the tomato sauce and allow time for it to thicken. If you add too much, you can thin it with more vegetable stock.

Biscuits

(MAKES 12–16 BISCUITS)

4 cups flour
2 tablespoons baking powder
¾ teaspoon baking soda
¾ teaspoon salt
1 cup (2 sticks) unsalted, sweet cream butter
1½ cups buttermilk

Mix dry ingredients together in a large bowl. Make sure butter and buttermilk are cold. Cut butter into ½ tablespoon–sized chunks and throw into flour mixture. Use a dough fork, butter cutter, two knives, etc. to cut the butter into the flour mixture. This can also be done with a food processor, by using the pulse mode, but don't overprocess. You want ¼- to ½-inch balls of butter.

When finished, pour in buttermilk and use a hard spatula to incorporate the buttermilk into the butter-flour mixture. Don't work the dough too hard, just enough to work in the buttermilk.

Lightly flour a clean, hard surface and pour out dough—it should want to fall apart. Using a dough cutter, begin collecting all the dough and shaping it into a rectangle. With a rolling pin, roll dough out to about ½ thick, trying to keep dough in a rectangle. Using a dough cutter, lift up one end of the dough and fold it back on itself. Roll dough out again to ¾ inch thick (a little thicker than before). Fold dough back on itself again and roll out to 1 inch thick, then cut biscuits. I use a pizza cutter to make square biscuits; you get less waste and avoid re-rolling the dough, which can make your biscuits tough.

Serve with tomato gravy, jam, or honey and butter.

Em's Restaurant

271 North Center Street
Salt Lake City, Utah 84103
(801) 596-0566
EMSRESTAURANT.COM
Emily Gassmann, Chef/Owner

Whether dining for lunch, dinner, or Sunday brunch, Em's menu of graceful and stylish foods keeps you coming back. Simple and refined, the ambience invites you in, and the food satisfies the hungry diner.

Chef/owner Emily Gassmann turned this historic facade, originally Center Street Market, into a room that feels as inviting as her home, with comforting smells coming from the kitchen and special care from the staff, all couched in the eclectic Marmalade neighborhood. Emily Gassmann's restaurant embodies the neighborhood bistro.

A restaurant's menu tells the diner details about the chef and what she values. Em's menu shows her personal style and touch in every dish, whether it's a perfectly poached egg sitting on crisp grated potatoes or well-cooked fish topped with sauce seasoned to perfection. High-quality, local ingredients are not a trendy boast or clever marketing plan. That's just how things are done in Em's kitchen. Every dish is polished to perfection.

You can see Em's deep enjoyment and passion for food by her well-worn cookbooks. This self-taught cook spends any down time she finds scouring through new and old cookbooks. She never leaves for vacation without a cookbook in hand, enjoying several newfound recipes during her break and returning with inspiration.

Though Em's Center Street spot feels like a hidden gem in Salt Lake, the real secret lies in the patio. Open in good weather, the patio overlooks the western mountains and is covered in vines and surrounded by beautifully potted plants. This is where you want to be on a cool summer night.

Em's provides a full dining experience. Alchemy Coffee sits next door, where you can grab a coffee before or after eating. Enjoy the Marmalade neighborhood while you're at it. Visit the capitol, walk through Memorial Grove or hike up City Creek Canyon for a full afternoon adventure along with a meal at Em's.

WILD SALMON OVER CREAMY CABBAGE

(SERVES 4)

½ head cabbage, sliced thin
2 tablespoons butter
2 tablespoons extra-virgin olive oil plus extra for
    cooking salmon
¼ cup red wine vinegar
½ cup heavy cream
Salt and pepper to taste
4 (6–8-ounce) salmon fillets

In a large skillet combine the cabbage with the butter and olive oil. Cook over low heat for 2 minutes, then add vinegar and cream. Simmer until cabbage is wilted. Season with salt and pepper to taste.

With a sharp knife score the salmon in a crisscross pattern, cutting through the skin and just slightly cutting into the flesh. Generously season both sides of the salmon with salt and pepper.

In a large nonstick skillet, heat the oil over moderately high heat. When hot, place the salmon fillets, skin side down, into the skillet. Cook without turning until the skin is very crisp, 2–3 minutes (cooking time will depend upon the thickness of the salmon). With a wide spatula turn the salmon over and cook for barely 30 seconds. Leave the salmon in the pan and remove it from the heat. The salmon will continue to cook as you prepare the plates with the creamy cabbage.

Spoon cabbage into the center of four warmed dinner plates. Top with a slice of salmon, skin side up, and spoon the warm sauce around the cabbage. Serve immediately.

Molten Chocolate Pots with Raspberry Sauce

(SERVES 5)

7 ounces dark chocolate

7 tablespoons butter, softened

⅓ cup sugar

4 eggs, lightly beaten

3 tablespoons all-purpose flour

For raspberry sauce:

1 pint raspberries

2 tablespoons sugar

Preheat oven to 400°F. Melt chocolate in a double boiler, then set aside. Place the butter and sugar in the bowl of an electric mixer and beat until thick and creamy. Gradually add the eggs and beat until smooth. Fold in the flour and melted chocolate. Spoon the mixture into five 4-ounce ramekins (greased and floured). Bake for 15 minutes.

To prepare raspberry sauce: Simmer fresh raspberries over low heat until they start to fall apart. Sweeten berries to taste with sugar (more or less to taste) and cook for an additional 2 minutes. As needed, thicken the sauce with cornstarch or thin with water. Top unmolded cakes with warm raspberry sauce.

CHOCOLATE IN UTAH

New research claims that Utahans were making chocolate before any other state in the union. But Utah can't take the credit. To be more specific, Utah wasn't even a state nor had Columbus sailed the ocean blue when the discovered chocolate was being made. The folks making chocolate were actually Ancestral Puebloan people near present-day Blanding, Utah, which is close to the four corners portion of Utah. Many locals are surprised to hear that in AD 750, on present-day Utah soil, Native Americans were paving the way for one of the largest industries in the world.

NATURAL HISTORY MUSEUM OF UTAH

To commemorate the incredible discovery and even more incredible cacao bean, the Natural History Museum of Utah (NHMU) put chocolate on display in early 2014 to show the city its place in the chocolate world. With a number of classes, seminars, and events, NHMU helped tell Utah about something far different and better than what they normally find in a Hershey's wrapper. Thanks to NHMU and the exhibit's main sponsor, Harmons Neighborhood Grocer, the narrative surrounding chocolate is changing.

Yes, it's a snack of sorts, but it's so much more. In the same way that wine and cheese is a deep, rich well of nuance to be studied and enjoyed, so is chocolate. Different chocolates taste differently depending on their origin and means of preparation. The NHMU exhibit united chocolate makers and lovers alike.

CAPUTO'S CHOCOLATE CLASS

Don't take our word for it. Take a class from Caputo's that explains on varying levels (beginner, intermediate, and expert) the story and science of chocolate. One of the best chocolate selections—in terms of quality and quantity—in the world lives on the shelves of Caputo's Market. Most of the fine chocolate–loving nation knows about Matt Caputo and his efforts to differentiate between "fine" chocolate and "standard" chocolate.

Salt Lake Magazine, a local authority on all things culinary, put Caputo's Chocolate Class on their SLC Bucket List. As the winds of change blow in Utah, much of the wind's origins are within the walls of Caputo's at their classes. In the beginner's class, the attendee is instructed on the things to look for, taste, hear, feel, and smell when determining if a chocolate is really good or if it's diluted with excessive vanilla and sugar. Most chocolate in the grocery store line is the latter. He's not saying that the massive chocolate brands are entirely bad (well, he kind-of is saying that). He is saying if that's your only experience with chocolate, then you've never actually experienced chocolate.

Caputo's classes have built a club of food geeks (their words, not ours) who surround local producers doing things the right way and support them in whatever way possible.

SOLSTICE CHOCOLATE

Scott Query is one such lucky recipient of the local scene's excitement and generosity. Scott and his wife, DeAnn, started Solstice after fifteen years of fascination with chocolate, all starting with the process and art of tempering chocolate. When Solstice started releasing bars, shelves carrying said bars were almost always empty due to demand. Scott discovered how to do, or more accurately, chose to do things that most respected the cacao bean and the person eating his chocolate. He sourced his beans responsibly and gave great care to every step of the process, much like a cobbler making fine shoes. Every detail matters. After only a short time in business, the Querys are experiencing praise from around the world for the chocolate coming out of their lab.

CHOCOLATE CONSPIRACY

AJ Wentworth of Chocolate Conspiracy is another leader in the chocolate charge in Utah. The Chocolate Conspiracy formed out of a love for nutrition obtained at the Tree of Life Rejuvenation Center in Arizona. During his time there he developed an "insatiable love of raw, vegan desserts." His primary focus within that was the cacao bean, which eventually inspired him to start his business crafting chocolate in old-world ways.

Chocolate in Utah is gaining steam and fans by the dozens. Yes, dozens. It's not a massive movement, but it's one rooted deep in quality and passion, where a handful of fans make chocolate at home much like the beer fan makes beer at home. Just like any other hand-crafted movement, growth is slow, but that's the way most artisans prefer it.

If you're looking for an elevated chocolate experience, head over to any one of these businesses, or try Liberty Heights Fresh, Harmons, or Whole Foods.

EVA

317 MAIN STREET
SALT LAKE CITY, UTAH 84111
(801) 359-8447
EVASLC.COM
CHARLIE PERRY, CHEF/OWNER

Small plates can too often be too small, too pricey, or boring. It's entirely unfulfilling to hunt for food after an evening of "small plates," and that's why Eva provides these small plates at affordable prices with flavor full enough to satisfy.

Locals quickly fell in love with Eva when it first opened because their small plate trend followed through with well-made, great-tasting food. Friends met up for dinner and enjoyed scooping bites off each other's plates and sampling new flavors. The more people at your table the more you get to try. The idea is to come and stay awhile. Eat, chat, then eat some more.

Popular plates include their brussels sprouts with hazelnuts, the oink oink oink (pork belly and pork loin wrapped in bacon), the French Pie (chicken wings topped with an egg and honey lime sauce), and the house-baked macaroni and cheese with bacon, tomato, and arugula.

Cocktails warrant attention at Eva too, with a boozy Sangria mixed with shiraz, brandy, citrus, peaches, thyme, and spices, as well as Eva's Whiskey, a wood-fired lemon muddled in Maker's Mark on the rocks.

As the popularity of brunch continues to rise in Salt Lake, Eva leads the way with an imaginative menu. Sweet potato hash, a waffled breakfast sandwich, and brunch *loukamades* stand out among other brunch menus in the city. The Benedict at Eva is unusual as well, made with chicken sausage, artichokes, and arugula.

Eva got its name from owner Charlie Perry's great-grandmother, someone who appreciated not only quality ingredients but also the pleasure of eating—an obvious value expressed at Eva.

Grab a few friends for a small plate experience in the heart of Salt Lake's historic Main Street.

Sautéed Brussels Sprouts with Toasted Hazelnuts and Cider Vinegar

(SERVES 6 AS A SMALL PLATE)

¼ cup hazelnuts

3 tablespoons butter

5 cups shaved brussels sprouts

Sea salt to taste

2–4 tablespoons (to taste) organic apple cider vinegar

To prepare hazelnuts: Preheat oven to 250°F. Place raw hazelnuts on a sheet pan and roast until you can smell them outside the oven, about 15–30 minutes. Peel the skins off the hazelnuts and cut them in half.

To prepare brussels sprouts: Heat a large sauté pan on high, then add butter and sprouts. Cook sprouts on high for 1–2 minutes, then add salt and hazelnuts and cook for 2–4 minutes on low heat. Finish with the cider vinegar and salt to taste. Serve warm.

Eva's Bakery

155 South Main Street
Salt Lake City, Utah 84111
(801) 355-3942
EVASBAKERYSLC.COM
Charlie Perry, Chef/Owner
Ryan Moore, Baker

A truly Parisian experience in Salt Lake City may sound like a contradiction, but we promise it's true. Eva's Bakery attracts attention from the start with its bright blue and yellow exterior and a sign announcing that it is a *boulangerie*, a word many locals may not know. Those who have been to France or have studied French know (and others can just smell the answer) that it's a place to buy bread.

Fresh bread hangs on the walls— from boules to baguettes. An espresso machine fills the room with the kind of white noise that you don't mind early in the morning. And glass cases tempt with beautiful, fresh-made baked goods and desserts. Sights, smells, and sounds allure at Eva's Bakery.

For breakfast the danishes, almond croissants, and lemon blueberry–stuffed french toast are just a few thoughts of what to enjoy. Lunchtime serves a variety of cravings, from pizza by the slice (or square in this case), soup, salad, and sandwiches. Grab food to go or have a lunch date, either work. Don't leave without dessert; the *canelé*, also known as "portable crème brûlée" persuades you to stay a bit longer; the vegan chocolate cookie is chewy, crisp, and rich all at the same time; and the goat cheese cheesecake is not only beautiful but creamy and decadent as well.

This bakery belongs to the owner of the tapas restaurant Eva, just down the street. Charlie Perry envisioned a true French bakery in Salt Lake City. His vision was born when in 1995 Charlie's grandfather, George Perry, purchased the infamous Central Milling (a highly reputable mill sourcing top bakeries across the western United States) in Logan, Utah, paving the way for bread-making in Charlie's future.

With the location of Eva's Bakery being in the heart of downtown, it provides the perfect outlet for those looking for a sweet pastry on their way into work, a quick bite at lunchtime, or a baguette to accompany dinner—a slice of Parisian life.

BLACKBERRY UPSIDE-DOWN CORNMEAL CAKE

(MAKES 9-INCH 1-LAYER CAKE)

For the caramel:

1 cup (2 sticks) butter
8½ ounces (1 cup plus 2 tablespoons) brown sugar

For the cake batter:

1 cup (2 sticks) butter
1 cup granulated sugar
5 whole eggs
1 egg yolk
1 cup plus two tablespoons (5 ounces) all-purpose flour
¾ cup (3.8 ounces) cornmeal
¾ teaspoon baking powder
¼ teaspoon salt
1 pint blackberries (about 2 cups)

To make the caramel: Combine the butter and brown sugar and cook on medium-high heat until sugar is dissolved and mixture turns a golden brown (be careful not to burn).

Line a round 9-inch cake pan with parchment paper. Pour caramel into the parchment-lined pan. Chill until the caramel is hardened.

To make the cake: Preheat oven to 375°F. Cream together the butter and sugar. Add eggs one at a time, then add the additional yolk. Sift together the dry ingredients, then slowly add them into the wet mixture.

Layer the berries on top of the caramel in the pan, then pour the cake batter on top of the berries. Bake for approximately 45 minutes to 1 hour.

Let cool then turn out onto a flat surface. Slice and serve at room temperature.

Downtown Farmers Market

Every Saturday from June to October, Pioneer Park turns into a gathering place and harvest celebration. The Downtown Farmers Market is more than just local food and fresh goods; it is where farmers and producers unite with the consuming community, food is exchanged, and friends are made.

If you're a regular at the market, you have your spots, like the farmer who grows lemon spinach and won't let you leave without a taste of his peaches, the stand with never-ending tastes of homemade jams, the guys making hummus so smooth you want to eat it by the spoonful, and the dried cherry guy whose cherries are perfectly tart and sweet. You find your favorites, and you visit them all summer long, stocking up your fridge with the best and freshest food in the land.

What you may not expect are the relationships you make along the way. You may find that the couple making the jam you love lives right around the block from you or that the guy making hummus loves his dog as much as you love yours. You may run into a coworker or old friend, and you'll certainly meet a few farmers who can tell you so much about their produce that you feel like you've been introduced to their child.

That's the beauty of the Downtown Farmers Market, or of any farmers' market for that matter. Relationships between producers and consumers cultivate and grow weekly, starting with just the exchange of a few dollars.

On hot days we like to cool off with a limeade from Sweet Salt Lake Fresh Mint Limeade. While the crew shakes up a limeade to go for you, buy some fresh mint limeade salsa.

Popsicles from Lick'd are also a good fit for late afternoon market-goers looking to cool off. Their flavors are unique and interesting, like plum basil or avocado pistachio.

For a snack, grab a bag of warm Pao de Quiju from Cheese Bread Mania. If you see a smiling cheerful lady working the booth, it's probably the owner, Deborah Hammond, showing her Brazilian pride.

For jam talk to Casee and John from Amour Spreads, and let them woo you with several silver-spooned samples.

For sorrel go to Chad Tagge Produce. Their sorrel makes a great potato soup and brightens up any salad.

Crumb Brothers makes the trek to the market with a truck full of bread. Get the baguette made fresh that morning.

Knight Family Honey brings a creamed honey to sample. Nearly all who sample leave with a jar in their bag.

Of course tomatoes are prevalent in late summer, and Tifi Ranch always has some colorful cherry-sized ones worth taking home.

For coffee the hot and cold brews coming from the Charming Beard Coffee booth satisfy in cool mornings and blazing hot afternoons.

Laziz Foods puts out the best spreads, from hummus to mahummara to garlic toum.

Slide Ridge makes a honey wine vinegar that now transcends Utah in popularity and demand. Pick up a bottle to make dressings, marinades, or sauces.

More to look for: fresh-made pasta, local bagels, olive oils, boiled peanuts, salami, kettle corn, local cheese, fresh meats, fresh fish, biscuits and gravy, and dried cherries.

Other than food you'll find jewelry, artisan crafts, dog food, plants, clothing, knife sharpening, soaps, and gifts abundant on the south side of the market.

The Downtown Farmers Market (slcfarmersmarket.org), sponsored by the Downtown Alliance, popped up about two decades ago and still somehow continues to be larger every year. Fight through the crowds and taste the best Utah has to offer.

HOMEMADE COLD BREW

If you walk around the Downtown Farmers Market, you'll find two or three booths serving cold brew coffee to hot, thirsty farmers' marketers. If it's the middle of the week and you find yourself wanting some cold brew, here are some tips from the gang at Charming Beard Coffee. There are a few ways to prepare cold brew coffee at home. If you don't have a Toddy Cold Brew coffeemaker, here is another way.

2 cups coarsely ground coffee (Blue Copper or Charming Beard is recommended)

4 cups cold water

Place the coffee grounds into a 4-quart pitcher, add the water, and stir until adequately combined. Cover with plastic wrap and steep at room temperature for 12–24 hours.

Line a strainer with a coffee filter and slowly pour the steeped coffee mixture through the strainer and into another pitcher or large bowl. Once you reach the coffee grounds at the bottom of the pitcher, stop pouring.

Discard the wet grounds, clean out the pitcher, and pour the cold brew back into the original pitcher. Cover the brew and chill in the refrigerator.

To serve: Fill cup with ice, pour two-thirds full with cold brew concentrate and one-third with water. Stir and serve.

Faustina

454 East 300 South
Salt Lake City, Utah 84111
(801) 746-4441
FAUSTINASLC.COM
Joe Kemp, Executive Chef

Joe Kemp came to town at just the right time. Chefs were in high demand, and the food scene was evolving and changing into something where a guy like him could find work. He moved from sous chef to chef de cuisine in two short weeks, and what was a vacation destination for his family quickly became home. Now he enjoys the mountains at a closer distance and a full-time gig at Faustina.

With Icelandic roots and an uncle working as a chef making Icelandic cuisine, Joe lets his background naturally influence his cooking. You'll find lamb and fish to be staples on the dinner menu, and dishes that guests enjoy regularly.

Brunch has become a Faustina highlight, and guests especially love the covered patio surrounded by tall pines, Japanese maple trees, bonsai bushes, and hanging flowerpots. Order a mimosa and their eggs Benedict over polenta and you'll be living the high life. For those with a sweet tooth, enjoy the cinnamon swirl pancakes drizzled with a cream cheese glaze and served with maple syrup.

Hillary Merrill, Faustina's general manager, makes sure to keep things warm and friendly, with an attentive and helpful staff. Coffee mugs are kept full and dishes brought out promptly.

Slip into Faustina, just like Joe did, and enjoy a well-cooked meal on a lazy weekend morning or special night out.

FAUSTINA'S EGGS BENEDICT

(SERVES 8)

For the polenta discs:

½ cup heavy cream
½ cup milk
1¼ cups water
½ cup polenta
2 sticks butter
¼ cup shredded Asiago cheese
¼ teaspoon chopped thyme
¼ teaspoon chopped rosemary
¼ teaspoon chopped sage
¼ teaspoon chopped basil
Salt and pepper to taste

For the hollandaise:

¼ cup white wine
1 teaspoon white wine vinegar
1 teaspoon minced shallots
1 tablespoon chopped fresh thyme
3 large egg yolks
1 cup (2 sticks) butter, melted
Juice from ½ small lemon
Dash of Tabasco
Honey, salt, and white pepper to taste

For the sausage:

⅓ pound ground Italian sausage

For the poached eggs:

8 cups water
2 tablespoons vinegar
4 large eggs

For the grilled tomatoes:

4 tomato slices (from 1 tomato)
Oil, salt, and pepper to taste

To prepare polenta discs: In a saucepan bring cream, milk, and water to a boil. Whisk in polenta and turn heat down to medium. Cook for 15–20 minutes, stirring occasionally. Fold in butter, cheese, and herbs. Salt and pepper to taste. Remove from heat and spread evenly on a sheet tray, so that the polenta stands about ½ inch deep. Cool, then cut into discs about 3 inches in diameter.

To prepare hollandaise: Combine white wine, vinegar, shallots, and thyme in a saucepan and bring to a boil. Reduce heat to medium and simmer until mixture reduces to two-thirds of original amount. In a separate bowl, whisk egg yolks for 7–8 minutes over a double boiler. Yolks should triple in size. Slowly drizzle in butter, lemon juice, Tabasco, and white wine reduction. Add honey, salt, and pepper to taste.

To prepare sausage: Sauté ground sausage in a skillet over high heat until thoroughly cooked.

To poach eggs: Bring water and vinegar to a boil. Drop eggs in and cook to preference.

To prepare grilled tomatoes: Lightly oil and season the tomato slices. Grill briefly on each side.

To assemble: Layer tomato, ground sausage, and eggs over the polenta discs. Cover with warm, fresh hollandaise.

FINCA

327 WEST 200 SOUTH
SALT LAKE CITY, UTAH 84101
(801) 487-0699
FINCASLC.COM
SCOTT EVANS, OWNER
PHELIX GARDNER, EXECUTIVE CHEF

True Spanish tapas have made their way to Salt Lake. Not the trendy American-style tapas that most often mean overpriced tiny plates with elaborate plating design, but authentic Spanish dishes served simply, as they should be, shareable and affordable.

For years Chef Phelix Gardner unknowingly has been letting the roots from his Spanish upbringing naturally guide his cooking. It wasn't until his undertaking at Finca that he realized that he had a natural bend toward Spanish flavors. Now, at Finca, they shine boldly in dishes like his Mejillones mussels with *sofrito*, Spanish chorizo and cava, and Smoked Chicken Croquetas with a piquillo puree.

Phelix was born in Spain and moved to the states when he was young. At the age of fifteen, Phelix got a summer job at a chain restaurant. Years later the job became more than something to pay the rent; it became something that propelled him into his career. He found himself cooking in big kitchens like the Peabody Hotel in Orlando, but when he found a job in Salt Lake, the slower pace of a smaller big city compelled him to move. "In Salt Lake you can focus on the food and feeding your customers well instead of always having to compete with the brand-new trendy restaurant," says Phelix.

Phelix is now the executive chef of both Finca and Pago, owned by Scott Evans. He's proud of his team at both restaurants, many of whom have matured within the business, going from pantry cook to grill cook and on to sauté cook. All are mastering the

house favorites, like the *albondigas* (lamb and pork meatballs) and the *papas y aioli* (potatoes with paprika and garlic aioli).

At Finca it's best to dine with friends. Bring those who enjoy sharing and order several tapas or a big skillet of paella, pass the dishes around, and get a taste of true Spanish cuisine. You'll each have your favorites, but it's likely there won't be a bite left when you're done.

SMOKED CHICKEN CROQUETAS

(SERVES 12-PLUS AS AN APPETIZER)

1 cup diced yellow onions

6 tablespoons butter

Salt to taste

1 cup flour

4 cups milk

2 tablespoons cream (optional)

1 smoked or rotisserie chicken, picked apart and
    shredded (meat only, no skin)

1 teaspoon thyme

1 teaspoon sherry vinegar

2 eggs

Flour seasoned with salt, pepper, and dried oregano

Seasoned bread crumbs

High flash point oil for frying

In a sauté pan soften onions in butter and season with salt. When onions are soft and translucent, add flour to create a roux. Whisk in milk and cream. Reduce heat to medium and continue to whisk as the sauce cooks.

When liquid comes to a simmer and is thickened, add chicken, thyme, and vinegar. Cook for an additional 5 minutes, while whisking, and then transfer to a sheet pan or bowl to cool. Cool in the refrigerator for at least 1 hour, or up to 2 days.

When you're ready to fry the croquetas, mix eggs with a splash of water to create an egg wash. Roll chilled filling into balls and dredge in seasoned flour, egg wash, and then seasoned bread crumbs.

Heat 1–2 inches of oil in a pan until almost smoking. Fry at 350°F until golden brown and warmed through, about 1–2 minutes per side.

FORAGE

370 EAST 900 SOUTH
SALT LAKE CITY, UTAH 84111
(801) 708-7834
FORAGERESTAURANT.COM
BOWMAN BROWN, CHEF/OWNER

The sound of Forage's praise resonates loudly through the valley, but if you're looking to dine there, you'll easily drive past it a few times before realizing it's the blue house next to the salon. It's perfectly unsuspecting. At first glance it appears merely a well-kept house, but upon entering it's a world-class food-meets-art dining experience sure to match the best of its kind anywhere in the country.

Few places capture a diner's imagination simply through plating, and then deliver even more on the flavor end of things, like Forage. Local chef star Viet Pham started Forage with Bowman Brown in 2009, which led to a well-deserved Best New Chef award

from *Food & Wine* magazine in 2011 for the two talents. Viet has since stepped out of Forage's kitchen to pursue other endeavors, leaving Forage exclusively as Bowman's canvas.

Forage offers a prefixed menu—the kind where you sit down, pay a flat rate, and enjoy every single bite from every course. Growing up in rural Arizona, Bowman says he was interested in growing food way before his interest in cooking. His nature-based approach to food warrants the name Forage as well as informs what he creates and how he creates it. Depending on the time of year, his menu changes considerably. A common winter menu might include sunchokes and apples, acorn and salted apples, cabbage and goat's

milk, or leeks roasted in coals. But one thing you can count on is Bowman's house-made granola to grab on your way out. This breakfast treat will keep you remembering your meal even the next morning.

Forage fits a perfect niche with very little competition in Salt Lake City. If you're looking for a prefixed menu with a dozen or more courses and top-notch wine pairings, Forage may be your only option around town. Salt Lake is still emerging as a great foodie city, and places like Forage and chefs like Bowman Brown (and formerly Viet Pham) are pushing it to the next level. When Forage started in 2009, it was ahead of the curve, and it remains that way today.

КОРЕНИЙ ГЛУБОКИЙ

ТРИ ЗВЕЗДЫ

Forage Granola

(MAKES 15 CUPS)

4 cups oats
3 cups chopped almonds
2½ cups chopped pecans
1½ cups coconut
2 teaspoons salt
¾ cup all-purpose flour
¾ cup (1½ sticks) butter
1½ cups maple syrup
1 tablespoon vanilla extract

Preheat oven to 325°F. Combine the oats, nuts, coconut, salt, and flour in a large bowl.

Toast the butter in a large skillet until browned and nutty. Let the butter cool a little, then slowly add the maple syrup and vanilla extract.

Combine the butter mixture with the oat mixture and mix thoroughly.

Spread the oat mixture out in one layer on a sheet pan (the granola cooks a lot better if it's in a nice thick layer on one sheet pan) and bake for 15 minutes. Rotate the pan and carefully stir the granola so the edges don't get too brown. Bake for another 20–30 minutes, stirring once if necessary, until the granola is uniformly browned all over. Let granola cool to room temperature. Store in an airtight container.

FRESCO ITALIAN CAFE

1513 SOUTH 1500 EAST
SALT LAKE CITY, UTAH 84105
(801) 486-1300
FRESCOITALIANCAFE.COM
MIKEL TRAPP, OWNER
LOGEN CREW, CHEF

Salt Lake City hosts plenty of beautiful restaurants that identify neighborhoods. At the classy intersection of 15th and 15th, tucked away but standing proud alongside Caputo's, the Paris, and the King's English, there's one such place that has been something of an anchor for the neighborhood for thirty years, Fresco Italian Cafe.

Walk down a brick path to a fairy tale–like vine-covered patio that leads inside Fresco where you'll be pleased to find a small dining room serving classic Italian dishes in an anything-but-predictable way.

What was once a home to a gas station and then a cafe known for its pot roast is now a small restaurant going thirty years strong.

Even in a dark room lit by candles and a fireplace with tables of white linen, this place somehow accomplishes accessibility—from the young diners saving the month's entertainment funds for a night out to the professionals on a casual date.

Chef Logen Crew was born and raised in Utah at a high school that paved a path to his culinary future. He competed in chef competitions and was mentored by top local chefs (most notably Chef Dave Jones of Log Haven). In gratitude for guys like Dave, Logen now mentors and coaches the kids in the same program.

While most of the food at Fresco alters seasonally, there are a few staples like the Fresco Polenta appetizer (wild mushrooms, pomodoro, pecorino-rosemary pesto) and the Chocolate Almond Crema for dessert. If it's fall you may see something like a sweet potato and chestnut ravioli topped with Brussels and Ricotta Salata. In the winter gnocchi topped with wild mushrooms may grace the menu.

No matter the season, Fresco serves up flavors worth savoring at a quiet table for a few hours with a perfect bottle of Italian wine.

Grilled Calamari with Fregola Sarda and Caper Salsa Verde

(SERVES 4–6)

For the calamari:

1 pound fresh calamari
½ cup chopped parsley
1 tablespoon chili flakes
4 cloves garlic, minced
½ cup extra-virgin olive oil
Salt to taste
Zest of 3 lemons

For the caper salsa verde:

8 ounces capers, rinsed
1 shallot, minced
2 cloves garlic, minced
1 tablespoon Dijon mustard
2 tablespoons red wine vinegar
¼ cup chopped parsley
¼ cup chopped oregano
¼ cup extra-virgin olive oil
½ teaspoon salt
Juice from the 3 zested lemons above

For the fregola sarda:

1 cup fregola sarda or Israeli couscous

Carrots, shaved for garnish

To prepare the calamari: Remove tentacles from the tube and set aside. Cut the calamari tube lengthwise and rinse out thoroughly. Remove any beaks or ink from the calamari tentacles and tube. If the tentacles are very large, cut in half. After the calamari is fully cleansed, rinse under cold water and then pat dry with paper towels until completely dry. Too much water on the squid will cause it to steam when cooking, which will potentially make the calamari rubbery. After the calamari is complete dry, mix with the rest of the ingredients and set aside to marinate.

Place a medium-sized sauté pan on very high heat. Once pan is very hot, put 1 cup of the marinated calamari into the pan. Make sure to give the squid a chance to sear before moving it around. After 2 minutes season squid with salt and a squeeze of lemon.

To prepare the salsa verde: Combine all ingredients in a food processor or blender and pulse until fully mixed. Check seasoning. Add more salt and lemon juice if needed.

To prepare fregola sarda: Following package directions, cook fregola sarda or couscous until tender.

To assemble: In a small saucepan place 8 to 12 tablespoons salsa verde with 2 to 3 cups cooked fregola and sauté until ingredients are combined and hot. Spoon directly onto four to six plates. Portion squid over the fregola and serve immediately. Shaved carrots are a nice garnish if desired.

Note: Fregola sarda is an Italian pasta made with semolina dough that is rolled into tiny balls and toasted in the oven. You can find this pasta at Italian import stores or specialty markets. Israeli couscous is a good substitute.

Gourmandise the Bakery

250 South 300 East
Salt Lake City, Utah 84111
GOURMANDISETHEBAKERY.COM
Verne Hanssen, Owner
Jean-Jacques Grossi, Chef

Not many chefs, when asked the question of how they got into food and cooking, answer with, "I had no choice." Jean-Jacques Grossi, chef at Gourmandise, fell into his career, but once you see the brilliant case of pastries at his bakery, you'll know it was no coincidence.

Jean-Jacques grew up in France with five brothers and sisters. To help out the family, he started an apprenticeship with his uncle in the food business in Le Lavandou, in southern France. He learned everything from charcuterie to pastry in his stint up against the Mediterranean Sea.

Years later his father, along with some of his siblings, moved to Salt Lake City. The opportunity for French cuisine in Salt Lake was obvious to his family, so Jean-Jacques followed, and he and his father quickly found themselves making an impact on French cuisine in Utah.

He has now been at Goumandise as the head chef for thirteen years and couldn't be more proud. The quality of the baked goods, along with the wide array of choices, showcases the hard work coming from his kitchen staff. "When people have a hard time choosing, you know you're doing something right."

The most popular desserts at Gourmandise are the napoleons, Almond Horn Cookies, Chantilly strawberry cake, Black Forest cake, and chocolate mousse cake. The bakery is also packed around lunchtime, as the downtown crowd visits for panini sandwiches and salads. Dinner and late night wine, beer, and dessert also prove their popularity; the parking lot at Gourmandise is never large enough for the crowds.

The secret to all this success—"consistency and dedication," says Jean-Jacques. Pastry and baking require a high level of attention to consistency and detail. Now Jean-Jacques chooses to use his gift to fill the shelves of Gourmandise with perfectly made treats.

ALMOND HORN COOKIES

(YIELDS ABOUT 20 COOKIES)

1 cup granulated sugar

1¾ cups (14 ounces) almond paste

½ cup egg whites (3 large egg whites)

1 teaspoon vanilla extract

2 tablespoons heavy cream (optional, see Note)

2 tablespoons flour (optional, see Note)

Sliced almonds

In a mixer, blend together sugar and almond paste until well mixed. *Slowly* add egg whites until mixture takes on a fluffy consistency. Add the vanilla extract, then the heavy cream and flour. Mix for 5 minutes or until smooth and creamy, with all ingredients fully incorporated.

Preheat oven to 350°F. Spoon dough or pipe from a pastry bag onto a parchment paper–lined cookie sheet (you may also use a greased cookie sheet or silpat). Sprinkle with sliced almonds.

Bake in preheated oven for 14–16 minutes or until just starting to brown around the edges. Do not allow cookies to brown.

Let cool completely before trying to remove cookies from parchment paper. If desired, cookies may be partially or fully dipped in chocolate.

Note: Omitting the heavy cream from this recipe makes it dairy free. Omitting the flour makes it gluten free. The gluten-free version is stiffer; dairy free is more fluffy; no flour or cream is more like meringue. For best results use both the cream and flour.

HARMONS NEIGHBORHOOD GROCER

135 EAST 100 SOUTH
SALT LAKE CITY, UTAH 84111
(801) 428-0366
HARMONSGROCERY.COM
BOB AND RANDY HARMON, OWNERS
AARON BALLARD, CITY CREEK COOKING SCHOOL HEAD CHEF
ALBERTO AGUILAR, CITY CREEK COOKING SCHOOL SOUS CHEF

What began as a fruit stand four generations ago now thrives as a Salt Lake City favorite employing 2,700 locals. Harmons provides families with a unique grocery experience and chefs with a unique career path.

The maze of Harmons City Creek awakens the imagination of the food lover with its aisles and aisles of colorfully organized grocery items, produce, and specialty products. On the top level of the store, a cafe serves quick lunch bites, coffee, and treats along with sushi and gelato. Sit and overlook the city while you enjoy an affordable and fresh-made lunch. The bottom level contains all the grocery items on your list as well as hot foods ready for dinner, a soup and salad bar, and a bakery to put all other grocery store bakeries to shame.

Fresh-squeezed tangerine juice, house-made buttercream on cakes, fresh guacamole, fifteen-plus cuts of chicken trimmed and ready for cooking, fresh-never-frozen fish, enthusiastic cheesemongers, checkout lanes with only healthy temptations, and its own cooking school all distance Harmons from its competition.

Aaron Ballard, head chef of Harmons' cooking school, landed himself quite the dream job for a chef, working normal hours and maintaining great work/life balance. Plus he has the largest selection of fresh foods just steps away from his work space. Students of his cooking school learn how to make homemade risotto, sous vide pork tenderloin, or other culinary challenges that push the home chef to a new level.

Bob and Randy Harmon, the brothers who now own Harmons, pride themselves on Harmons continued relevancy given its eighty-plus years in business. "Food is fuel. It directly affects your health," says Bob. Clean, real, healthy food isn't just hype at Harmons; their passion and motivation is clearly on display in every corner of the store.

Quinoa Cranberry Salad

(SERVES 4–6)

For the quinoa:

1 cup red quinoa

1 cup white quinoa

½ cup ⅜-inch-dice red onion

½ cup ⅜-inch-dice red bell pepper

½ cup ⅜-inch-dice green bell pepper

½ bunch of cilantro, finely chopped

1 cup frozen corn, thawed

¾ cup dried cranberries

½ cup drained and rinsed black beans

For the dressing:

¼ cup oil

¼ cup red wine vinegar

½ cup honey or agave

1 teaspoon salt

½ teaspoon black pepper

½ teaspoon minced garlic

To prepare salad: Bring two stockpots with 8 cups of water in each to a boil. Add the red quinoa to one pot and the white to the other and boil. Cook until the quinoa sprouts, then cook 2 additional minutes, approximately 10 minutes for the white and 12 minutes for the red. The white will take less time, so be careful not to overcook. Drain quinoa and lay out on cookie sheets to cool.

In a large bowl combine the onions, peppers, cilantro, corn, dried cranberries, and black beans with the cooled quinoa.

To prepare the dressing: Whisk the dressing ingredients together. Toss dressing with quinoa, mixing well.

HELL'S BACKBONE GRILL

No. 20 North Highway 12
Boulder, Utah 84716
(435) 335-7464
HELLSBACKBONEGRILL.COM
Blake Spalding and Jen Castle, Chefs/Owners

Few restaurants can say both the drive to the restaurant and the vegetables they serve will bring you to your knees. Divine scenery and food collide at this literal farm-to-table destination. Drive through otherworldly, breathtaking views of Escalante canyon country that lead you to the remote town of Boulder and Hell's Backbone Grill, a peaceful gathering place that encourages visitors to revere something greater than themselves.

As you walk up to the restaurant, you get a sense that a gathering has just taken place. Chairs beside an old wooden table out front are left slightly pulled out, showing frequent use. Wine sits at the bar, ready for a pour, and you may just meet one of the farmers or ranchers on your way out.

Providence brought Blake Spalding and Jen Castle together. And together they came up with a revolutionary, old-world experience that inspires a new wave of dining in the southwestern United States. The two friends bought some farmland and started a restaurant. The six acres of land now provide over 12,000 pounds of produce per year for

the restaurant. They would love to sell more of it at the Downtown Farmers Market, but they truly make use of every pound during the season they're open. If you do see Blake or Jen at the market, buy a cookbook and make a reservation.

Eat at Hell's Backbone Grill today and you will find many dishes showcasing the season's best as well as their local meat. They even have their own rancher, Katie Austin, who provides lamb for the restaurant, like in this recipe.

Friends and folks curious about the restaurant concept come from all over to get the full experience. They dine, hike, fish, relax, and dine again, becoming part of the congregation of Hell's Backbone before they leave. The simplicity of life and food here is one that draws en masse, and sends you away feeling more peaceful than when you arrived.

HOPI LAMB STUFFED PEPPERS

(SERVES 8)

8 red bell peppers, one-quarter of a side carved off to create a pepper boat, green stem intact

1 pound ground lamb

½ onion, finely chopped

2 tomatoes, roughly chopped

3 cloves garlic

2 teaspoons thyme

1 teaspoon red pepper flakes

½ teaspoon cayenne (optional)

2 tablespoons salt

1 tablespoon pepper

2 cups cooked posole corn (may substitute 1 [28-ounce] can whole white hominy, drained)

½ cup warmed honey

1 cup toasted piñons (pine nuts)

1 egg, slightly beaten

1 cup Pepper Jack cheese, cut into 1-inch cubes

Remove all seeds and membranes from the peppers. Steam red peppers to soften, 7–10 minutes over boiling water. Set aside.

Preheat oven to 350°F. Sauté ground lamb and onion in a large skillet over medium heat until onion softens and meat is browned. Add tomatoes, garlic, spices, salt, and pepper and cook for 1 more minute. Transfer to a large mixing bowl.

Add drained posole corn, honey, and piñons to the bowl and stir well. Adjust seasonings to taste. Toss in the beaten egg and cheese cubes.

Spoon filling into pepper boats, heaping slightly. Place in a greased 9 x 11-inch baking dish, nestling the peppers to fit snugly. Bake for 25–35 minutes, until peppers are soft, filling is hot, and tops are starting to crisp.

High West Saloon

703 Park Avenue
Park City, Utah 84060
(435) 649-8300
HIGHWEST.COM
David Perkins, Owner
James Dumas, Executive Chef

Driving up Parley's Canyon to Park City for dinner from Salt Lake City feels like a treat to some and punishment to others. At one point the Park City brand told SLC dwellers that for great food and drink, Park City was your only option. On the other hand, SLC loyals thought it blasphemy to give Park City the respect of the long drive and steep bill. Salt Lake has come a long way. Somehow the city—once considered less than sophisticated—keeps locals from feeling the need to drive through the Wasatch Mountains for a night out.

Now High West Saloon is calling Salt Lake City-ites back up the mountain.

Yes, High West primarily distills and blends whiskey. If you don't live in Utah, that's probably the reason the name sounds familiar. David Perkins started High West to be a playground for his whiskey ideas, and in his brilliance led the distillery to open a flagship restaurant that matches well the western aesthetic of his whiskeys. High West Saloon compels the urbanite to not only take the drive up to the Saloon, but also to come back regularly.

For every High West whiskey you try there waits another equally as interesting and tasty. The same goes for the menu at the Saloon. Chef James Dumas is to food what David Perkins is to whiskey. Perkins takes a common product in whiskey and somehow reinvents it by boiling it down to its simplest form. Dumas matches the innovation-through-simplicity mindset with his High West Signature Burger, a bison-beef-blend burger with aged gruyère, blue cheese, and caramelized onion tucked between a caraway bun. You'll also see it in the High Country chicken pot pie or the fried polenta.

Whether it's the whiskey or the food, High West makes Utahans proud and for good reason.

WHISKEY BRAISED SHORT RIBS

(SERVES 4)

1 tablespoon blended oil

12 short ribs

Salt and pepper

1¼ pounds mirepoix

3 tablespoons butter

1 tablespoon chopped garlic

1¼ tablespoons kosher salt

6 tablespoons all-purpose flour

5 quarts water

1 (28-ounce) can peeled tomato

6½ tablespoons canned chipotle, divided

1 cup Ancient Age Whiskey, divided in half

½ cup vermouth

3 cups apple cider

1 tablespoon demi-glace

1 tablespoon beef stock

Heat blended oil in a large pot, roasting pan, or dutch oven over high heat. Tie off the short ribs and season with salt and pepper. Sear ribs until dark brown on all sides, then remove browned ribs and set aside.

Pour all fat out of the first pot, then add the mirepoix and sauté for 5 minutes, until light brown. Turn heat down to medium, 350°F, and add butter and chopped garlic. Stir until butter is melted, then add salt.

Sprinkle flour evenly into skillet and mix well with vegetables, garlic, and butter. Add water and scrape the bottom of the pan, then add the tomatoes, 5½ tablespoons of the chipotle, ½ cup of the whiskey, vermouth, cider, demi-glace, and stock.

Bring to a boil, then turn down to simmer. Add ribs back in and turn heat to low, 250°F. Cook for 4 hours (possibly 5). Remove ribs from pan and place into a serving dish. Leave all vegetables in the pan.

Boil the liquid down to 2½ quarts, or half of the original liquid, and skim off the fat, then add additional ½ cup Ancient Age and remaining 1 tablespoon chipotle. Using an immersion blender or transferring mixture to a blender, blend the sauce until smooth.

Strain sauce and serve over ribs immediately or chill. At High West these ribs are served with fried polenta and red onions.

Note: A mirepoix is a mixture of chopped of carrots, onion, and celery. Demi-glace is a rich brown sauce used in French cuisine. You can find it at specialty stores or can try making it at home.

Lamb's Grill

169 South Main Street
Salt Lake City, Utah 84111
(801) 364-7166
LAMBSGRILL.COM
Frances Liong, Owner
Vladamir Guerrero, Executive Chef

The oldest restaurant in Utah, Lamb's Grill, takes the waves and trends of local dining in stride. Under new ownership with Frances Liong, the classic restaurant has gotten even classier and more accessible to Utah diners.

You'll still find a place to hang your hat and coat at every booth. Red leather chairs that twist at the base welcome those hoping to dine at the counter. Art deco threaded mirrors give you a reflection of the past. You're simply taken back in time when you dine at Lamb's. Listen to Frank Sinatra's "Fly Me to the Moon" while you sip a classic Manhattan cocktail and await Lamb's Beef Bourguignon before you go to the theater.

Lamb's originally opened on George Washington's birthday in Logan, Utah, under the care of a Greek immigrant in 1919. George P. Lamb moved his restaurant to the business district of Salt Lake City in 1939. It resides there still, in the historic Herald building that once housed the Herald newspaper. You'll still find a picture of George Washington in the main dining room, given to George Lamb by the mayor at the opening of the restaurant.

Braised lamb shanks, lentil soup, and rice pudding remain favorites at the restaurant. A few menu items have been added, like the new favorite of bacon-wrapped blue cheese–stuffed dates, and a few have been taken away, but regulars know the secrets to dining at Lamb's. Though it's not on the menu, you can still order sautéed calf liver and onion, a dish that to modern diners may not seem appetizing, but for those who have been dining at Lamb's for years, it's a favorite.

Generations dine at Lamb's. What was once the hippest place to grab a bite to eat outside of the home has now become a spot where memories are recalled and made new. Recently an older gentleman embarrassingly waited in his car as his daughter walked into Lamb's to pay back her dad's $5 tab from when he dined and dashed decades ago. Grandparents take their grandchildren here for classic breakfasts, and anniversaries are celebrated. Memories.

"Lamb's is not a stuffy place to come. There's a lot of trendy places around town, but you can't buy history," says owner Frances Liong.

Lamb's Beef Bourguignon

(SERVES 10–12)

1 teaspoon extra-virgin olive oil

2 ounces bacon, chopped

5 pounds chuck tail, cut into large cubes

2 large carrots, medium dice

3 stalks of celery, medium dice

4 ounces pearl onions

2 cloves garlic

2 cups red wine

2 ounces tomato paste

1 teaspoon dried thyme

1 tablespoon chopped dried rosemary

3 bay leaves

½ tablespoon salt

1 teaspoon pepper

¼ cup flour

1 cup demi-glace mix

Water to cover

Put oil and bacon into a large dutch oven or tall-sided, ovenproof sauté pan. Place on medium heat and cook until bacon is rendering off some fat, but not all the way cooked, about 4 minutes. Add the chuck tail cubes and sear, turning the heat up. After searing the meat (a couple of minutes on each side), remove it from the pan and set aside. Add carrots, celery, onions, and garlic. Sauté on medium heat for 10 minutes or until carrots are soft. Remove and set aside.

Deglaze the pan with red wine, using a wooden spoon to get any stuck pieces loose from the bottom of the pan. Add tomato paste, thyme, rosemary, bay leaves, salt, and pepper. Mix to combine. Return meat and veggies to the pan. Add flour, demi-glace, and water to cover the meat and veggies by 1 inch.

Cover pan with lid and place in a 275°F oven for 4½ hours.

Laziz Foods

LAZIZ-FOODS.COM
(435) 757-9310
MOUDI SBEITY AND DEREK KITCHEN, OWNERS

It's a luxury to like the people who make your food as much as you like the food they make. It's ideal, but in our hyper-processed world of fast food we rarely think of our producers as knowable let alone likable. Laziz Foods marries great Lebanese food with responsible ownership, which comes together to make Utah proud and the food community hungry.

Moudi Sbeity and Derek Kitchen are partners in business and life, championing admirable causes across the board—marriage equality, public transportation, pet adoption, and just about anything else that makes Utah a better place to live for everyone. However, their food warrants attention on its own merit. That's what makes this such an ideal marriage. One taste of Laziz Foods and you'll see that clearly it stands on its own.

Laziz began with hummus at the Downtown Farmers Market in Salt Lake City, and news of the creamy, simple ingredients spread across town, quickly inspiring ethnic food fans across the board to taste and see the real deal. No added oils and no preservatives tell Utahans the story that great food is made from natural ingredients and when it's made locally, preservatives are unnecessary. At the farmers' market you can taste, purchase, and meet the guys who make the food you'll likely consume entirely when you get home.

After the success of the hummus, Laziz Foods moved forward with *muhummara* (roasted sweet red peppers, pomegranate molasses, and walnuts) and eventually *toum*

(a Lebanese garlic spread). It likely won't stop there either. Anything from Moudi's native Lebanon is up for consideration. The more Utahans gain a taste for it, the deeper Moudi will go into his culture's recipes.

Derek and Moudi are partially riding the wave and partially driving the car that is elevating Utah's food from expected to unexpected, boring to interesting and memorable.

TOUM VINAIGRETTE

(MAKES 1 CUP DRESSING)

⅓ cup vinegar (we used Slide Ridge Honey Wine Vinegar)
¾ cup extra-virgin olive oil
1 teaspoon *toum* (add more depending on taste)
½–1 teaspoon black pepper
Salt to taste

Blend all ingredients with an immersion blender. Serve on salad, over pasta, in a sandwich, or as a dip.

ETHNIC MARKETS

For imported groceries there is a variety of stores—small to large—selling unique goods.

The Oriental Market, Ocean Mart, and South East Asian Market are great spots to find Asian imports, from ingredients to make homemade *pho*, to unusual vegetables, kimchi, miso, spices, fresh herbs, sauces, and even *mochi* ice cream.

Pars Market offers Persian cuisine and groceries, including dates, rice, beans, and spices like saffron.

At Rancho Market you will find a food court with a bakery as well as a variety of Mexican imports. The marinated meats and chile verde are not to be overlooked, and the *chicharron* torte is worth the visit alone.

For Eastern European goods check out Black Cherry Market, where you can find Russian chocolates, European sodas, imported yogurt and kefir, grape leaves, and lots of unusual candy.

The Japan Sage Market carries kombu, *togarishi*, *furikake*, and many other Japanese favorites.

Shop N' Go is the place to go for Indian and Pakistani foods like spices, rice, beans, *dosa* batter, and sauce mixes.

Most markets also carry ready-to-eat prepared foods like *kimbap* at Oriental Market, roasted pork and duck at Southeast Market, samosas at Shop N' Go, and Mexican pastries at Rancho Market.

ETHNIC RESTAURANTS

No one would expect it, but Salt Lake City has a thriving ethnic food scene. With a large population of refugees, return missionaries, and a decent amount of daring diners, there's a growing demand for more diverse foods.

You don't have to go far to find Ethiopian food, where diners can enjoy eating (with their hands!) a variety of meat stews, lentils, and other braised vegetables, all gathered up in traditional sourdough sponge bread, *injera*. Try the African Market on Redwood or Blue Nile on State Street.

You don't have to have a cold to enjoy a big bowl of *pho*, though it's like medicine if you do. Pho Tay Ho resides in a small house on Main Street and serves up delicious *pho* daily. Oh Mai offers up MSG-free *pho* as well as Vietnamese *banh mi* sandwiches.

Though Utah tends to be a little bland in flavor, the Indian food restaurants don't tone it down for locals. Himalayan Kitchen, Saffron Valley, and Bombay House are the local's favorites for authentic Indian cuisine.

Chanon Thai offers up traditional Thai food in a simple atmosphere, giving you a glimpse into Thai culture.

And if you want to hop on the dim sum train for brunch, stop in at New Golden Dragon and bring friends.

Les Madeleines

216 East 500 South
Salt Lake City, Utah 84111
(801) 355-2294
les-madeleines.com
Romina Rasmussen, Chef/Owner

When words like buttery, flakey, and rich define a bakery's most popular pastry, it must be good. Les Madeleines is known for their Kouing Aman, a well-kept secret recipe originating from Brittany, France, with magic in every bite. And while crowds flock for the pastry, locals know that the menu teems with worthy compositions and offerings. French macarons, unusual cookies, croissants, and of course madeleines are also favorites alongside a great number of sweets.

Romina Rasmussen, a local to Salt Lake, traveled around the world post–pastry school at the French Culinary Institute to find inspiration for her little bakery. The result is a rich assortment of tastes from abroad. Bringing back her experiences and her desire to share them with Salt Lake gives us all a bite of something beyond our borders.

Her Sesame Chicken Wrap, served for lunch, takes you right to Asia, where she found inspiration from the flavors on her visits. This gluten-free wrap is served wrapped up in butter, lettuce, and rice paper, giving a good crunch with every bite. And you'll want to make sure you dip the wrap into the miso dressing for the perfect accompaniment.

Pomme frites inspired by her French exploring and sandwiches named after their flavor-profiled cities (Paris and Madrid) make a worthy addition to your Salt Lake bucket list. On a cold winter day in Utah, nothing quite hits the spot like Romina's chicken pot *pithivier*, her French take on the classic chicken pot pie.

The famous Kouing Aman, recognized by *Food & Wine* and the Food Network, is simple yet complex, sweet yet salty, layer upon layer of gasp-worthy goodness. Romina describes it as "a study in opposites." So don't let the caramelized crunchy exterior fool you; buttery soft pastry awaits in the center, making every bite a perfect balance.

With a courageous and amiable owner, Les Madeleines has brought fame and flavor to Utah. Let's all toast our buttery pastry to Romina.

MATCHA MADELEINES

(MAKES 12 MADELEINES)

⅞ cup all-purpose flour (1 cup minus 2 tablespoons)

½ cup plus 1 tablespoon sugar

1 pinch salt

½ teaspoon baking powder

½ teaspoon matcha (Japanese green tea)

2 eggs

½ cup (1 stick) unsalted butter, melted

Combine all dry ingredients in the mixing bowl of a stand mixer with the whisk attachment. Whisk all dry ingredients for about a minute to evenly incorporate. Add the eggs and mix on high for about 5 minutes. With the mixer on a medium speed, add the butter in a slow, steady stream. When it is fully incorporated, turn up to high and mix for 5 more minutes.

Chill the batter overnight.

Transfer half of the dough into a pastry bag. Pipe out the matcha batter into a buttered/floured madeleine mold or muffin tin. Bake at 375°F until they bounce back (12–14 minutes). Then repeat with remaining batter.

Unmold immediately. Serve bump side up.

SESAME CHICKEN WRAP

(MAKES ABOUT 12 WRAPS)

For the sesame chicken wrap:

1 whole chicken (3–4 pounds), cooked and shredded

3 scallions, white and green parts thinly sliced, no roots

¼ bunch cilantro, roughly chopped, no stems
  (about ⅓ cup)

1 tablespoon toasted sesame seeds

Sesame mayo to taste (see recipe)

Salt and pepper to taste

1 head butter lettuce

70mm rice paper

For the sesame mayo:

1 cup mayonnaise

1½ teaspoons sesame oil

For the miso dressing:

1½ cups white (shiro) miso paste

6 tablespoons sugar

6 tablespoons mirin

½ cup hot water

4 teaspoons soy sauce

1½ teaspoons sesame oil

2 tablespoons rice vinegar

Black and white sesame seeds, for garnish (optional)

To prepare sesame mayo: Whisk together mayonnaise and sesame oil until smooth.

To prepare sesame chicken wrap: Combine chicken, scallions, cilantro, and sesame seeds, then add enough sesame mayonnaise to make it as creamy as you like. Salt and pepper to taste.

Separate the butter lettuce leaves, rinse, then pat dry with a paper towel. Put approximately ¼ cup sesame chicken salad into a large butter lettuce leaf and place a smaller leaf on top.

Dip a sheet of rice paper into hot water for about 5–10 seconds or until sides start to curl up. Place the rice paper on the counter or on a cutting board. When it has softened, place the lettuce in the middle and fold the bottom and top of the wrapper up over the lettuce. Fold over one side, tucking in the edge. Roll to complete the wrap. Repeat with the rest of the chicken salad.

To prepare miso dressing: Put all ingredients in a food processor and blend. Serve alongside the wraps with black and white sesame seeds sprinkled on top.

LIBERTY HEIGHTS FRESH

1290 SOUTH 1100 EAST
SALT LAKE CITY, UTAH 84105
(801) 467-2434
LIBERTYHEIGHTSFRESH.COM
STEVEN ROSENBERG, OWNER
KATE ROBINSON, PASTRY CHEF

One conversation with Steven and you'll see that he's always a little ahead of the curve. He's got a long list of ideas and an even longer history with Salt Lake City. A film student from Michigan State, Steven had hopes of being in the film industry on one level or another. After some time on task and a few reality checks, Steven found himself in Salt Lake City at the corner of 1290 South 1100 East operating Liberty Heights Fresh.

At the time, a specialty market of Liberty Height's caliber showed one part vision and perhaps a few parts insanity. In 1994 Utah sat entrenched in bizarre liquor laws and odd restrictions, leaving the food scene in a constant position of limbo. On many levels Steven

was in an uphill battle, but one that eventually paved the way for a thriving specialty food scene in Salt Lake City.

Spend an afternoon in Liberty Heights Fresh and you'll see a special caliber of customer who knows about local farms, understands cheese on a higher level, and asks questions that you'd never hear at your local supermarket. Steven's market simultaneously created the need for an elevated quality of home ingredients and satisfied it for Liberty Height's loyal base.

Liberty Heights isn't cheap (because fine ingredients aren't cheap), and you won't find Steven apologizing for that any time soon. In fact, he uses the critique of his prices to have the bigger conversation: "We spend significantly more on health care than we do food. If we spent more money on better food with less chemicals and preservatives, then our need for health care would reduce greatly."

Idealists like Steven are the grease for the wheels of change. Steven laid much of the foundation on which the local food scene stands with said grease. Many ought to be thankful.

CHÈVRE BROWNIES

(MAKES 12–16 BROWNIES)

For the brownies:

1 cup (2 sticks) plus 2 tablespoons butter, divided

6 ounces chocolate (preferably 60 percent cacao)

1¼ cups all-purpose flour

¼ cup plus 1 tablespoon cocoa powder

¾ teaspoon salt

3 eggs

1 cup sugar

1½ teaspoons vanilla extract

For the chèvre topping:

¼ pound chèvre

½ egg, beaten (about 2 tablespoons)

2 tablespoons cream

2 tablespoons sugar

To prepare brownies: Preheat oven to 350°F. Butter and flour an 8 x 8-inch or 9 x 9-inch pan. Line with parchment paper and grease that as well.

Melt butter and chocolate in a double boiler. Combine flour, cocoa powder, and salt in a separate bowl.

In a mixer with the paddle attachment (the paddle attachment gives the brownies a fudgy texture), combine the eggs, sugar, and vanilla. Beat until light and fluffy. With the mixer on low, slowly add ¼ cup of the melted chocolate and butter mixture to the egg mixture. Continue adding chocolate ¼ cup at a time. Beat until all the chocolate is combined into the egg mixture.

Add the flour mixture and beat on low until just combined, scraping the sides of the bowl as needed. Pour into prepared pan.

To prepare chèvre topping: Combine chèvre, egg, cream, and sugar in a bowl and whisk until smooth and creamy. Pour the topping over the brownie mixture and swirl with a knife or spatula to create a marbled top.

Bake for about 45–55 minutes or until firm in the center. Cover the pan with foil for at least the first half of baking to prevent the chèvre topping from burning. Let cool, then slice and enjoy!

LA NAY FERME

Clinton Felsted knows technology, not farming. At BYU he started a company that afforded him the money and time to give to a vision for better food in Utah. Take a walk with Clinton around the farm and you'll hear his passion and vision delivered in a way resembling Ray Kinsella's distant looks and compulsion to build a baseball field in the middle of an Iowa cornfield.

So why did Clinton start La Nay Ferme? He believes in food. Better food, to be more specific. He aims to generate a better relationship between people and their food. Even people of means eat garbage because they don't understand food. Clinton believes that everyone should spend time on a farm seeing how things are grown and understanding the work of the farmer. Take a look at the list of ingredients on the back of a pre-made salad from a grocery store or chain restaurant and you'll come across a list of ingredients that even your high school chemistry teacher is unfamiliar with. Then eat from a La Nay Ferme CSA and taste what vegetables straight from the ground taste like. It's a far cry from what most Americans eat daily.

La Nay Ferme is a force for good in a world where food is more often created in a laboratory than by the sweat of an honest farmer. Visit a farm sometime and see what food really looks like.

MARY MALOUF

Her house screams Austin, Texas, with its loud colors and weathered boot collection, but her work, sometimes with obscenities, speaks for itself. Her spunk, fearlessness, and decades of experience as a food writer combine to make Mary's work deep and interesting, and at times you think, "Can she really say that?" The answer is yes.

Local foodies know Mary as a food writer for *Salt Lake Magazine* who was crowned editor in 2014. She's the face and force behind the Salt Lake Dining Awards, which are the most meaningful awards for local restaurants. The annual event is a who's who of local dining culminating in the announcement of Best Restaurant. Even if local restaurateurs try to play it cool and act like the awards are meaningless, no one has ever turned down their award, and every winner proudly hangs the award near the entrance of their restaurant.

Salt Lake City found gold when Mary moved to town. She's a mainstay of the local food scene and an advocate for its success while demanding that it be great. Steven Rosenberg from Liberty Heights Fresh says, "Salt Lake City doesn't really understand how great we've got it having Mary Malouf as a writer in our town." We agree. In due time, we suppose.

Log Haven

6451 East Millcreek Canyon Road
Salt Lake City, Utah 84109
(801) 272-8255
LOG-HAVEN.COM
Margo Provost, Owner
David Jones, Executive Chef/Owner

Turn your phone off at the bottom of the canyon, take a deep breath, and prepare for an evening of solace and refreshment. Log Haven is, and has been for decades, giving folks rest from the fury of everyday life. The streams, waterfalls, and abundant nature surrounding the restaurant have a mystical healing that inspires visitors to faithful visits.

This haven began as a home in the 1920s—a man's gift to his wife. The home was transformed into a restaurant, and at some point the beloved spot lost its attraction, leaving the home with little hope but to be destroyed. That's when current owner and good Samaritan, Margo Provost, came in to rescue this gem. With dedicated determination and what she calls a stewardship to the land and the community, she invested all of her personal wealth in the hopes of renewal and restoration.

Today Log Haven is owned by a team of four who may as well be family, with Margo as the matriarch. The allegiance that they each have to the home and business is evident, and the care shines through in every detail, from the food to the service and ambience.

David Jones, an owner and the executive chef of Log Haven, lives and breathes the surroundings in his cooking style. He blends the old with the new in a complex yet rustic menu. Plans for a native edible garden excite Dave, as he hopes to create a closer connection with the land and food.

Log Haven continues to be a gathering place even beyond its use as a restaurant. People gather for weddings, private events, and to make memories with loved ones. Many destination restaurants tend to focus more on the environment and less on the food, but at Log Haven meticulous attention is given to both. Earthy foods like forest mushrooms and horseradish parsnips perfectly reflect the rustic atmosphere. Sit by the window with a view of the snow and mountains, enjoy tunes of a bygone era coming from the piano, and taste flavors you'll be recalling for years to come.

Whether visiting for a wedding, romantic dinner, or post-hike hors d'oeuvres, Log Haven has a way of enchanting guests and removing them from a plugged-in life to one of digital freedom, if only for a night.

FROZEN COCONUT SOUFFLÉ WITH ROASTED PINEAPPLE SAUCE

(SERVES 12)

Step 1:

12 egg yolks
⅔ cup sugar
3 tablespoons water
2 tablespoons agave nectar

Place the egg yolks in a mixing bowl. In a saucepan heat sugar, water, and agave nectar to 238–242°F (soft ball). Remove the syrup from the heat and whisk it slowly into the yolks, making sure to not allow the yolks to curdle. Whip the yolk mixture until the yolks have doubled and cooled to room temperature; set aside.

Step 2:

4½ cups heavy cream
1 vanilla bean, split and scraped
2 tablespoons banana compound (available from specialty food stores, or substitute 2 teaspoons banana extract)
2 tablespoons sweet coconut cream (or substitute coconut cream)
3 ounces coconut rum

With a mixer, whip the cream, vanilla bean, banana compound (or banana extract), coconut cream, and coconut rum to a soft peak. Chill until needed.

Step 3:

2½ tablespoons water
½ cup sugar
4 egg whites
¼ teaspoon cream of tartar

In a medium saucepan over medium heat, bring the water and sugar up to 238–242°F (soft ball).

While the sugar is cooking, start whisking the egg whites and cream of tartar in a clean mixing bowl.

When the sugar syrup reaches "soft ball" stage, remove it from the heat, turn the mixer up, and slowly pour the sugar syrup into the whites. Increase the speed to high until the whites start showing signs of soft peaks. Turn the mixer to medium speed and continue whipping until the whites form a firm peak.

Step 4:

12 (6–8-ounce) plastic cups
2–3 cups toasted coconut

Place a tablespoon of toasted coconut on the bottom of each cup, reserving remaining toasted coconut for unmolding and plating.

Step 5: Pull together the soufflé:

⅓ cup shredded coconut
Yolk mixture from above
Egg whites from above
Whipped cream mixture from above
12 prepared souffle cups (see step 4)

Fold the shredded coconut into the yolk mixture, then fold the coconut-yolk mixture into the whites, then gently fold in the whipped cream. Evenly spoon soufflé batter into the prepared cups and freeze for at least 8 hours.

To serve: Simply unmold the cups and roll the outside of the frozen soufflé in the remaining toasted coconut. Serve with the roasted pineapple sauce (see recipe).

Note: These soufflés are not baked but frozen into a custard-like dessert. The eggs are safe to eat following these instructions.

For the roasted pineapple sauce:

1 small pineapple
Fresh lime juice
Cornstarch or flour

To prepare roasted pineapple sauce: Heat oven to 325°F. Remove top from pineapple. Place whole pineapple on a baking sheet and roast for approximately 1½ hours, until soft and sugary. Remove the outer skin and core and roughly chop the pineapple fruit.

Puree the cooked pineapple in a blender with a squeeze of fresh lime juice. Remove the pineapple puree from the blender and strain into a saucepan. Check for sweetness. If the pineapple was roasted at a ripe stage, it will not need any sugar. Otherwise you may need to add a little simple syrup or agave nectar.

Heat the pineapple puree to a simmer and check the viscosity. If the sauce is too thin, you may need to thicken it slightly as follows: In a separate bowl mix a small amount of starch (like cornstarch or flour) with a bit of the puree, stirring to make sure there are no lumps. Add slowly as needed to the simmering puree until the desired viscosity is reached.

Chill the puree until serving time.

Tea-Brined Pork Tenderloin

(SERVES 2)

2 (14-ounce) cleaned pork tenderloins
2–3 tablespoons grape seed oil

For the tea brine:

1 quart warm water
2 tablespoons salt
⅓ cup agave nectar
1 quart cold water
2 tablespoons whole white pepper
2 sliced oranges
2 sliced lemons
2 sliced limes
1–2 sprigs rosemary
3 tablespoons ground juniper berries
½ cup white wine
1 cup very strong brewed Oolong tea

Huckleberry Gastrique (see separate recipe)

To prepare tea brine: Dissolve the salt and agave nectar into the warm water, then add the remaining ingredients. Allow the brine to set overnight in the refrigerator for maximum saturation of flavors before adding the meat. Add the pork and allow to brine in the refrigerator for approximately 6–8 hours.

To prepare meat: When ready to cook the meat, remove the tenderloin from the brine and pat the meat dry with a cloth or paper towel. Preheat oven to 375°F.

Heat grape seed oil in a medium sauté pan and sear the pork on all sides until golden brown. Finish cooking the tenderloin in the oven for 5–7 minutes or until desired temperature (medium is 145°F using a meat thermometer).

Let the pork rest for 5 minutes before slicing, then drizzle with Huckleberry Gastrique.

HUCKLEBERRY GASTRIQUE

(SERVES 2)

4 tablespoons sugar

1 tablespoon water

2 tablespoons rice wine vinegar

½ cup huckleberries, pureed in a food processor or blender

2 tablespoons apple juice

1½ teaspoons fresh lemon juice

½ teaspoon Dijon mustard

1 sprig lemon thyme

¼ cup whole huckleberries

1–2 tablespoons brandy or cognac (optional)

Salt and white pepper

In a heavy saucepan caramelize the sugar and water by cooking the sugar over medium-low heat. Once it reaches a nice amber color, carefully add the rice wine vinegar and cook out any lumps by constantly stirring.

Add the pureed huckleberries, apple juice, and lemon juice and reduce until the sauce coats the back of a spoon when lifted.

To finish the sauce, add the Dijon mustard, lemon thyme, whole huckleberries, and brandy. Season with salt and white pepper to taste. Continue to reduce on low heat if needed, until sauce reaches the desired consistency.

Note: At Log Haven this dish is also served with quinoa and roasted acorn squash.

LUGANO

3364 SOUTH 2300 EAST
SALT LAKE CITY, UTAH 84109
(801) 412-9994
LUGANORESTAURANT.COM
TYLER STOKES, EXECUTIVE CHEF/CO-OWNER

When you think of an acclaimed fine-dining Italian restaurant, with white tablecloths, perfectly folded napkins, and a fire burning in the fireplace, you probably don't also think about indie rock and snowboarding. Tyler Stokes, music aficionado, snowboarder, and family man, is the head chef and part owner of Lugano. Tyler learned to cook Italian food in the Lugano kitchen alongside its original owner, Greg Neville. Eventually he made his way up the ranks and became part owner after a journey moving around and opening reputable places of his own.

Tyler had many stints working at other restaurants, including ownership of a restaurant in Sun Valley named Dashi. All the while he stuck to ski towns where the powder could be enjoyed on days off.

As a new partner of the business, Tyler foresees great changes while still keeping with the legacy of simple Italian cuisine. He hopes to take Lugano into the future with a more modern appeal, local ingredients, and heightened presentation.

Though the menu may undergo some fresh changes, the most popular dishes remain the Spaghetti with Cauliflower, red curry clams, beef carpaccio, baby beet salad, and their homemade pastas and ravioli.

It's an exciting time to be at Lugano and even more exciting to be in Tyler's kitchen. The kitchen staff listens to indie rock, blues, and anything with heart and soul to inspire the team. "This helps us in the kitchen," says Tyler.

This Salt Lake Italian food staple is experiencing a rebirth with Tyler Stokes.

SPAGHETTI WITH CAULIFLOWER AND NAPA CABBAGE

(SERVES 4)

1 head cauliflower, blanched

4 ounces extra-virgin olive oil, divided

1 pound imported spaghetti

4 ounces pancetta, cut

4 cloves garlic, sliced

Red chili flakes (optional)

Salt and pepper to taste

1 cup sliced napa cabbage (or a large handful)

1 ounce Parmesan

2 ounces ricotta salata, for finishing

To blanch the cauliflower, first remove the florets from the head and chop into smaller pieces. Prepare a large pot of boiling water with a pinch of salt and a large bowl of ice. Cook the cauliflower in boiling water, covered, for 3 minutes. Drain and place cauliflower in the bowl of ice. Once cool, drain the ice and water and set cauliflower aside.

In a separate large pot, bring water for the pasta to a boil. Add salt and 1 teaspoon (¼ ounce) olive oil. Place 1 pound spaghetti in the boiling water, stirring occasionally to prevent pasta from sticking. When cooked through, drain spaghetti and set aside.

In a large sauté pan, add 2 ounces olive oil and 4 ounces pancetta. Cook over medium heat, occasionally stirring pancetta until it becomes slightly crispy. Add sliced garlic. Continue to stir until garlic is lightly browned. Add blanched cauliflower pieces, red chili flakes, salt, and pepper. Continue to cook for an additional minute. Lastly, add cabbage and toss together. Pull the pan off the heat.

Immediately add cooked pasta to the cauliflower mixture. Toss together. Add Parmesan and additional olive oil to achieve desired consistency. Divide among individual plates. Garnish with grated ricotta salata.

Meditrina

1394 South West Temple
Salt Lake City, Utah 84115
(801) 485-2055
MEDITRINASLC.COM
Jen Gilroy, Chef/Owner

Two gals set out to bring something new to Salt Lake City, bringing small plates and a high-quality wine list to an urban neighborhood. Jen Gilroy and Amy Britt put their heart and souls into making Meditrina a fabulous place for locals. With pride and determination they mapped out their concept, then patiently waited three years to have their wine bar placed in a neighborhood. Because they found the building in pretty rough shape, they put a lot of blood, sweat, and tears into transforming it, leaving only three fruit-stamped tiles as you enter the kitchen as a remembrance of the building's past.

Jen and Amy recently parted ways—Amy opened up her own restaurant, Pig and a Jelly Jar—but the style and passion behind Meditrina remains. Jen, originally from Vernal, Utah, found her food roots in the South when she went to business school in Nashville, Tennessee, at Belmont University. She put herself through school waiting tables at Italian

and fusion-style restaurants. Now the roles are reversed as she finds music to be more of a restorative pastime and the restaurant business to be her full-time career.

At Meditrina guests dine looking for full-flavored bites, unique wine pairings, and a comfortable dining experience. Every second Tuesday of the month, Jen hosts Wine Social Night, with themed wine pairings like Latin food and wine, or rosés for the early summer months. Many guests become regulars, having a standing reservation for every second Tuesday.

For the curried shrimp Jen's tip is to watch the prawns carefully so as not to overcook. If they've curled up, they're overdone. Cook them in a hot pan and remove just slightly before they're done, because they'll continue cooking even after you remove the pan from the heat.

MEDITRINA'S CURRY LIME PRAWNS

(SERVES 2 AS AN ENTREE OR 4–6 AS AN APPETIZER)

1 tablespoon yellow curry powder

2 teaspoons cumin

½ teaspoon cayenne

¼ teaspoon dry ginger

1 tablespoon sugar

½ teaspoon salt

3 tablespoons fresh lime juice

1 tablespoon butter

1½ cups half-and-half

¼ cup extra-virgin olive oil or canola oil

1½ pounds peeled, deveined prawns

In a small saucepan over medium heat, combine all the spices, sugar, salt, lime juice, and butter and whisk over medium heat until butter is melted. Add half-and-half, bring to a boil, then reduce to a simmer for 3–5 minutes. The sauce should be a little lighter than the color of yellow mustard. Remove from heat.

In a large sauté pan, add oil and allow pan to get hot over medium-high heat before adding the prawns. Sear both sides of the prawns just until pink (about 2–3 minutes per side). Add curry lime sauce and simmer until prawns are done. (Remember—overcooked shrimp are not happy shrimp!)

Serve over basmati rice for an entree or cucumber slices for an appetizer.

LONG-DISTANCE DINNERS

There are more than a handful of places worth a little driving to dine at. Load up your car with friends and a few small snacks and hit the road for a little adventure.

Drive east to Midway, a small Swiss town outside of Park City, for some great Mexican food at Tarahumara. An extravagant salsa bar, chile verde–smothered burritos, and *tres leches* cake await.

Drive north to the little town of Eden and you'll find several gems, from southern barbecue to Mexican food and the oldest bar in Utah.

Only twenty minutes south, in Draper's old town, a little cafe is waiting to be discovered. Food for Thought serves breakfast and lunch in a cozy turn-of-the-century home.

At Bonneville Brewery, beers and burgers topped with cheese and onion rings make the drive to Bonneville worthwhile.

Though there are many restaurants worth the trek up to Park City, a few lesser-known finds make a day trip more interesting. Try Reef's Mediterranean, Good Karma, and Deer Valley Grocery Cafe.

Provo also has some worthwhile gems like Black Sheep, Communal, and Pizzeria 712.

If you want a really quirky adventure, drive out to Oakley to dine in an old art-deco-styled train car, the Road Island Diner, where comfort food reigns.

And if a four-hour trip can still be counted as a long-distance dinner, Hell's Backbone Grill in Boulder and Cafe Diablo in Torrey must make it on your list.

TACO CARTS

On the corner of State Street and 800 South, the hungry taco fan finds the best value in town. Though Sears looms just beyond the parking lot with value aplenty, the better value sits in its shadows. Two taco carts with dirt-cheap tacos and burritos sit on the corner and combine to make what some locals affectionately call the Sears Food Court.

Tacos Don Rafa and Toro have served two tacos for $1.50 as long as most locals can remember. It's not just ground beef and chicken either. No, they serve far more than the gringo favorites. At these carts you can get lingua (tongue), *cabeza* (head), and many other authentic Mexican meats bent on finding flavor where many Americans shamefully turn their noses.

Avoid these carts when the lines are at their longest—lunch, dinner, and when the bars across the street close. Drive by during these times and see lines that most restaurants envy.

Mezzo Drinking Chocolate

990 South 700 West, Suite 8
Salt Lake City, Utah 84104
MEZZOCHOCOLATE.COM
Topher Webb, Owner

Topher Webb started Mezzo Drinking Chocolate out of a genuine love of Oaxacan culture, style, and approach to drinking chocolate. In Oaxaca, making drinking chocolate straight from the cacao bean transcends socioeconomic boundaries as a drink shared by all at most every celebration. It's a drink that unites and supports the great milestones and rites of a culture. This depth and richness and flavor inspired Topher to start Mezzo Drinking Chocolate.

A culture rich with cacao finds many uses for the great bean, all putting on display the magic and alchemy held inside. American culture finds ways to do as little as possible to sell something as legitimate or the "original." What Americans call "hot chocolate" bears almost zero resemblance to the drinking chocolate from which it derives. Most hot chocolates have trace amounts of cacao and disproportionate helpings of sugar and vanilla and a list of other ingredients in need of a chemistry degree to understand.

Topher is joining the chorus of voices in Salt Lake City championing a better way. He could easily purchase inexpensive cacao made on farms that do little to support their farmers and their families. With today's wordsmith marketing strategies, he could cut corners and still call it the genuine drinking chocolate. But if you go to a tasting at Mezzo or spend an afternoon with Topher, you'll see that his style and approach honor the cacao bean, the farmer, and Oaxacan tradition. He sources single-origin beans, meaning all the cacao in a particular bag comes from one country, one region, one farm, and one harvest.

With meticulous attention to detail from farm to warehouse to cafe, Mezzo is telling a new story of an old tradition.

MEZZO'S CHOCOLATE HORCHATA

(SERVES 6–8)

1⅓ cups uncooked long-grain white rice

5 cups water

2 cups whole milk

1 cup heavy cream

1 (14–ounce) can unsweetened coconut milk

6¼ ounces Mezzo Chocolate La Red 80 percent

⅔ cup sugar

½ vanilla bean, split and scraped

½ tablespoon vanilla extract

1 tablespoon ground canella (Mexican cinnamon)

Place uncooked rice and water in a blender. Blend together until rice starts to break up, typically about 2 minutes. Pour water and rice in a pitcher with a lid and let stand at room temperature for a minimum of 4 hours.

While rice is steeping in water, place milk, cream, and coconut milk in a saucepan. Bring to a simmer over medium heat, being sure to stir to keep milk and cream from scalding. Once mixture starts to simmer, remove pan from heat and stir in chocolate with a wire whisk. Mix well. Pour mixture through a wire strainer into a pitcher and set in the fridge to chill.

When rice is done steeping, pour the rice through the strainer into the blender once again. Pour the chocolate mixture from the above paragraph into the blender as well; add sugar, vanilla bean, vanilla extract, and canella and blend on low until well incorporated. Pour back into the pitcher, preferably with a lid, and place in the fridge until very chilled.

Note: Chocolate *horchata* is best when served in a chilled glass. *Horchata* is a drink enjoyed with particularly spicy meals in Mexico to cool the palate. The addition of chocolate adds a wonderful depth that pairs well with meals using mole poblano, mole negro, or any traditional red enchilada sauce. For a fun twist steep a little orange zest in with the milk in the second step.

NAKED FISH BISTRO

67 West 100 South
Salt Lake City, Utah 84101
(801) 595-8888
NAKEDFISHBISTRO.COM
Sunny Tsogbadrakh, Executive Sushi Chef

Call Naked Fish, make reservations, and request *omakase*. That's the first thing you need to do when planning an evening at Naked Fish. Chef Sunny Tsogbadrakh knows far better than you the best selections in his kitchen on any given day. Trust him. When going the route of *omakase*, you surrender everything you think you want and simply tell the chef, "I'll leave it to you." No menus, no wavering back and forth on what to get or what to avoid. Chef Sunny dials it up for you at his discretion.

Naked Fish flies its fish in all the way from Tokyo, making several trips to the airport throughout the week. Most of their fish is killed *ike-jime*, which involves spiking and killing

the fish quickly, preventing reflex in the muscles and thus leaving a stress-free fish. And a stress-free fish means a better, softer-flavored fillet. According to the general manager, Christian Frech, this is one of the most humane methods of killing fish.

Even if you don't want to give all control over to Sunny, it's a good practice to surrender for just one order of nigiri or sashimi. Oftentimes they'll even bring you a cut of the fish that is more unusual than you've ordered before—like salmon belly or salmon shoulder. And the same rules apply whether it's pork or fish; the belly and shoulder are always a good bet.

Thanks to fresh wasabi, perfectly seared scallops, crispy shishito peppers, and, of course, the sake menu, Naked Fish ravishes guests and invites them to stay awhile. Great restaurants are the sum of compelling food, good vibes, apt environments, and hospitality. At Naked Fish a wonderful synergy of all these components grace the guest with a night worth remembering.

Hamachi Tataki

(SERVES 2)

5 ounces sashimi grade hamachi, cubed

1 cucumber, thinly sliced

1 jalapeño, thinly sliced

1 ounce green onion, thinly sliced

For the sauce:

½ ounce rice wine vinegar

4½ ounces miso

1½ ounces sugar

1 ounce mirin

¼ ounce grated ginger

2 teaspoons lemon juice

2 teaspoons lime juice

Mix all sauce ingredients together. Add hamachi, cucumber, jalapeño, and green onion to sauce.

Garnish with ginger blossom and serve over Japanese milk leaf (if available).

Note: Sunny's tip is to soak the green onion in water to take away some of the strong flavor. He also likes to use dehydrated cucumber.

No Brow Coffee Werks

179 West 900 South
Salt Lake City, Utah 84101
(801) 222-7046
NOBROWCOFFEE.COM
Joe Evans, Founder
Duffy Gallivan, Owner

No Brow Coffee Werks' founder, Joe Evans, and specialty coffee have become interchangeable words in Salt Lake City. For the better part of two decades Joe has served the tired, thirsty, and early risers of Salt Lake City great coffee from roasters from around the country. In 2006 Joe founded No Brow in hopes of elevating the local coffee scene.

Early No Brow fans frequented the shop in its 3rd and 3rd location near Gourmandise and the old Atlas Architects office. Far from their beginnings in the

humble (though large) warehouse-type room that lacked consistent heating and air-conditioning, you'll now find Joe and owner Duffy Gallivan in the up-and-coming neighborhood of Central Ninth. The Redevelopment Agency of Salt Lake City currently invests much of its resources into the neighborhood in hopes of revitalizing it. No Brow sits in the middle of the efforts as a notable operation to draw other businesses.

No Brow carried a lot of momentum in their 3rd and 3rd location. Joe said the move came from a need for a better building, one that better fit the coffee they serve. On the No Brow shelf you'll find local specialty roasters Blue Copper and Charming Beard Coffee alongside Intelligentsia (based in Chicago), Ritual (San Francisco), Commonwealth (Denver), and others in an ever-changing roster rotation of great coffees.

Most coffee shops have a shelf of synthetic flavors lining the walls—blueberry, vanilla, hazelnut, and the list goes on. No Brow generally likes to keep it pretty basic and pure. After all, their goal is to source great coffee, so why dilute it with heavy synthetic syrups? Let the coffee speak for itself. That said, they offer a house vanilla simple syrup free of the high-fructose corn syrup and preservatives one usually finds in such flavors. It's simple and tastefully done, much like No Brow Coffee Werks.

No Brow's Wassail

(SERVES 10–12)

2 cups water
½ cup sugar (unbleached organic)
4 allspice berries
8 cloves
2–3 cinnamon sticks
1¾ cups orange juice
¾ cup lemon juice
1 quart apple juice

Combine water, sugar, and spices in a large pot or crock pot and bring to a simmer. Add in fresh juices. You can leave the wassail on the heat, ready to serve, or chill it and reheat at your convenience; it should keep for a week or more.

Note: No Brow uses fresh-squeezed citrus in the shop. They strain the whole mix through a fine mesh sieve.

I got a version of this recipe from my mother, and she got it from hers. Everyone in the family puts their own twist on it (I use fresh juice and more orange/less lemon), and my aunt adds pineapple juice. I've had people mention that they have had a similar version with apricot nectar. It's a fun recipe to mess with. and there's no right or wrong way to do it, just be mindful not to scald it. If you like a little more punch to it, reduce the water by a little and serve it with a splash of bourbon or brandy.

SPECIALTY COFFEE

As with every sub-scene that exists under the dining banner, specialty coffee is rising.

Stumptown started a new wave for coffee in 1999 along with Intelligentsia and Counter Culture in the category largely dominated by Starbucks. Cultivating a thirst for ethically traded beans and superior presentation, taste, and conscience in roasting and sourcing, coffee's third wave found a home in Utah.

Local roasters like Charming Beard Coffee Roasters, Publik, and Blue Copper along with aesthetically pleasing and coffee connoisseur favorites like No Brow Coffee Werks, The Rose Establishment, and Cafe D'Bolla all work together to elevate Utah's coffee scene to a level that Utah residents from ten years ago wouldn't even recognize. Who would have thought that cups of coffee would sell for $5 and twelve-ounce bags of whole beans for $25? Salt Lake City's embrace of specialty coffee takes a perfect snapshot of Utah's elevating scene.

Oasis Cafe

151 South 500 East
Salt Lake City, Utah 84102
(801) 322-0404
OASISCAFESLC.COM
Efren Benitez, Head Chef

Over eighteen years ago, a young guy named Efren Benitez moved from Vera Cruz, Mexico, to Salt Lake City and got a job washing dishes at Oasis Cafe. He knew no English and had never stepped into a commercial kitchen before. He didn't even cook at home; he always found a way out of it when his mom would ask him to help with the cooking.

Now Efren's mom, still in Mexico, can hardly believe that her son is the head chef at a top restaurant in Salt Lake City. Efren made his way from dishwasher to head chef all in the Oasis Cafe kitchen. On occasion he now calls his mom for tips on some of her classic Mexican dishes. While Oasis Cafe serves mostly American cafe-style cuisine, they do have a few modern takes on Mexican dishes, like their mole fajitas or chicken and goat cheese tamales.

Efren finds much of his success working alongside a great team in the kitchen. He often suggests an idea, and they all come up with the final product together. Creative dishes are being born all the time at Oasis. For brunch they serve a salmon chorizo with their huevos rancheros, and for dinner they have a new risotto seasonally.

The risottos at Oasis aren't your typical risottos. Sweet corn risotto with blackened chicken and avocado salsa, root vegetable risotto with smoked hickory sauce, and wild mushroom risotto with applewood smoked bacon and a poached egg are just a few examples of unorthodoxy. Efren mentions that the key to making good risotto is that the rice should still be soft before the cheese and butter are added. This way the flavor will shine through best.

Brunch, lunch, and dinner are all available at Oasis, and when the patio is open, it may just be the best spot to dine in town. And with a story like Efren's, you can't not enjoy Oasis Cafe.

WILD MUSHROOM RISOTTO

(SERVES 6–8)

For the risotto base:

½ small white onion, diced
¼ cup vegetable oil
2 cups white wine
2 cups Arborio rice
2½ quarts vegetable stock (hot) or water

For the scallion butter:

¾ pound scallion tops, chopped finely
1 cup (2 sticks) unsalted butter, at room temperature
¼ teaspoon salt
Pinch of ground black pepper

For the wild mushroom risotto:

½ cup (1 stick) unsalted butter
4 ounces vegetable oil
14 ounces wild mushrooms (any type)
24 ounces risotto base
36 fluid ounces water
12 ounces scallion butter
6 ounces Parmesan cheese, grated
Salt and pepper
6–8 poached eggs, depending on how many people
    you're serving
3 ounces crispy applewood bacon, diced
2 ounces white truffle oil
1 ounce chives, chopped finely

To prepare risotto base: Sauté the onion in oil until it begins to turn soft and clear. Add the wine and cook over a low heat, until the onion is falling apart and the wine has evaporated. Add the rice, mix well, and then begin adding broth, a ladle at a time, stirring gently all the time. When the rice has almost reached the al dente stage, remove the pot from the fire. Place rice on a sheet tray and allow to cool.

To prepare scallion butter: Blanche the scallions (put in boiling water for 30 seconds, remove and dunk in ice bath, then transfer to a new bowl). Place scallions, butter, salt, and pepper into a blender (make sure butter is at room temperature) and blend at high speed until smooth. Remove from blender and refrigerate for at least 2 hours or until hard.

To prepare wild mushroom risotto: Add butter and oil to a large hot sauté pan. Add mushrooms and cook until slightly crispy. Add risotto base and water, stir well, reduce heat to medium, and simmer until water is reduced. Remove from heat. Add scallion butter and cheese; mix well until blended. Add salt and pepper to taste.

Divide into individual bowls and top with one poached egg, diced bacon, a sprinkle of truffle oil, and a pinch of fresh chives.

OH MAI

3425 SOUTH STATE STREET
SALT LAKE CITY, UTAH 84115
(801) 467-6882
OHMAISANDWICH.COM
LONG TRAN, OWNER

Slightly outside of Salt Lake City proper, Oh Mai displays a menu worth the drive. Its *banh mi* sandwich and delicious *pho* are nothing short of an accomplishment in flavor, culture, and quality.

With the presence of the Mormon Church (and thus return missionaries), Utah's demand for extra-cultural cuisine is surprisingly unexpected, to say the least. One look at the landscape of Utah and one might stereotype the cuisine in Utah as typical, bland, and more of an endeavor of convenience than passion. But places like Oh Mai tell a different story to those not convinced of Utah's diversity in cuisine.

Oh Mai specializes in the traditional *banh mi* sandwich, which is something of a combination of French bread (culturally adapted and adjusted to a Vietnamese style) and Vietnamese ingredients. One bite into a *banh mi* at Oh Mai and your mouth comes alive with flavors of raw or pickled vegetables, some sort of oven-roasted or pan-seared meat, and fresh cilantro. The freshness of *banh mi* knows few equals in the sandwich world.

To wash it all down, Oh Mai serves up a tasty Thai iced tea. It's orange. It's tannic. It's creamy. It's worth every sip and slurp.

Though Oh Mai is small when it comes to square feet, its reputation around the city is huge. All discussions of ethnic food in Utah quickly turn toward this small restaurant on State Street in South Salt Lake City. The environment is nice, the service is good and efficient, but again, these are not the things that draw Oh Mai fans to wait in a line going out the front door and into State Street. It's the food.

FRESH SPRING ROLLS

(SERVES 8, 2 SPRING ROLLS PER PERSON)

4 ounces rice vermicelli
2 cups shredded lettuce
2 cups thinly sliced cucumber
1 cup thinly sliced carrot, fresh or pickled
1 cup thinly sliced diakon radishes, fresh or pickled
2 bunches green onions
16 (8½-inch diameter) round rice paper sheets
1 pound shrimp, cooked, peeled, and sliced in half
Optional herbs: cilantro, mint, and basil

Bring a medium saucepan of water to a boil. Boil rice vermicelli for 3–5 minutes or until al dente, then drain.

Prepare the vegetables by roughly chopping the lettuce and slicing the cucumber, carrot, and radishes. Cut the white ends off the green onions and slice in half lengthwise.

Fill a large bowl with hot water. Dip one rice paper wrapper into the hot water for a few seconds to soften. Lay wrapper on a flat surface. In a row across the center, place 2–3 shrimp halves, a small handful of vermicelli, lettuce, cucumber, carrot, and radishes. Add in a couple of long green onion slices. Leave about 2 inches uncovered on the top end. Fold over the top end, fold one side over the shrimp and vegetables, then tightly roll the wrapper. Repeat with remaining wrappers.

PAGO

878 SOUTH 900 EAST
SALT LAKE CITY, UTAH 84102
(801) 532-0777
PAGOSLC.COM
SCOTT EVANS, OWNER
PHELIX GARDNER, EXECUTIVE CHEF

Scott Evans runs deep. He's been in the restaurant business long before his first ownership endeavor, Pago. Anyone who's been in the restaurant industry in Salt Lake City for the past two decades either knows Scott, worked with him, or knows someone who knows him. He's like the Kevin Bacon of the Salt Lake City restaurant scene.

Around the time of Pago's opening in 2009, the ground underneath Salt Lake City's restaurants had started shifting. So many local restaurants were satisfied and comfortable with their current condition, leaving much to be desired by the new foodie movement that was slowly making its way to landlocked Utah. Eating was transitioning from the thing one did before going to a movie to the thing one does *instead* of a movie. Yes, there absolutely were great restaurants around the city at the time and long before, but Pago entered at about the time Salt Lake foodies started demanding something better, something fresher and more seasonal than the average Utah restaurant offered.

Scott Evans saw the desire for better ingredients and local sourcing from ethical farms swelling in Utah before Utahans really even knew what it was or what to call it. Soon after Pago's opening, the term "farm to table" was the phrase of choice around town. In Utah it makes perfect sense to marry the restaurant table to the local farmer. In fact, it's a shame that it took so much work and education to open the public's eyes to the truth that the food we eat should come from farms. Outside of the greater Salt Lake City area, northern Utah is fairly rural and farm-heavy.

With farms aplenty and an increased demand for something on par with the coastal food centers, Pago opened up in the 9th and 9th neighborhood and gave reason for the locals to be proud. It certainly wasn't the first great restaurant in Utah, but, somewhat intangibly, it (along many other notable establishments mentioned in this book) marked the beginning of the food revolution in Utah.

Pago keeps the term *farm to table* fresh. The menu is honest, and Chef Phelix Gardner fits perfectly into Scott's scheme. Pago's concept and execution will transcend the trends and remain an important spot in Salt Lake City for years to come.

Kale Caesar Salad

(SERVES 4–6)

2 bunches kale

For the Caesar dressing:

2 tablespoons whole-grain mustard
3 egg yolks
2 tablespoons grated Parmesan cheese
2 tablespoons minced garlic
2 tablespoons capers
2 tablespoons lemon juice
½ tablespoon kosher salt
1½ cups oil

Optional dressing supplement:

1 tablespoon chopped anchovy
1 tablespoon finely chopped garlic
¼ cup extra-virgin olive oil

For the fried sunchokes (use fingerling potatoes as a substitute):

2–3 sunchokes
Peanut or other frying oil

For the pickled fennel:

1 cup apple cider vinegar
¼ cup water
1 tablespoon sugar
2 teaspoons salt
1 bay leaf
2 cloves
2 fennel bulbs

To prepare Caesar dressing: Combine all ingredients, except oil, in a food processor or blender. Puree until ingredients are pulled together. Slowly drizzle in oil to emulsify. Add any of the dressing supplements as you wish or use the anchovy as a garnish.

To prepare sunchokes: Thinly slice sunchokes (about ¼ inch thick), then fry at 300°F. If using fingerling potatoes, you may fry them or bake at 375°F for about 10 minutes.

To prepare pickled fennel: Combine all ingredients, except fennel, in a pot and bring to a boil. Core fennel and shave on a mandoline or slice thin. Transfer fennel to a small pan or bowl. Pour boiling pickling liquid over fennel and let sit overnight.

To assemble the salad: Chop the kale into bite-sized pieces, removing and discarding the stems. Dress the kale in about half the dressing (reserving the rest for later use). Add in some of the pickled fennel and toss to combine. Garnish with crispy sunchoke chips and extra anchovies.

Pallet

237 South 400 West
Salt Lake City, Utah 84101
(801) 935-4431
EATPALLET.COM
Buzz Willey, Head Chef

A little flare of Portland sits on the fringes of downtown Salt Lake City. A couple of entrepreneurs—Rocky Derrick and Drew Eastman—banded together to renovate an old warehouse space into something of a destination for its design alone. Locally designed lighting with a nod to the industrial revolution, eye-catching art hung in perfectly random order on the walls, mismatched glass pitchers alongside dark-stained wood tables, and an old-world-style bar give Pallet an atmosphere worth making a visit.

The building formerly housed Salt Lake's first creamery, where wooden platforms were once loaded into trucks, hence the name Pallet. There's no escaping the double entendre of the creamery's pallets and the palate on which Chef Buzz Willey sees a canvas.

Buzz chose the path less traveled according to his family line, not venturing into business but instead into his individually found passion of food. His grandmother sparked his interest in cooking, and he would cook with her at family holiday gatherings while the other kids would be outside playing. His individuality continued when he dropped out of college for culinary school, letting his heart lead the way. And today his heart guides his cooking still, as he enjoys bringing fresh fish, seasonal dishes, and high-end cooking to downtown Salt Lake.

When you sit down to eat, you'll immediately be drawn to the art on the walls. Co-owner Rocky Derrick's wife, Courtney, painted each oil painting herself, each speaking to the era of the building. The dark aura around the room creates the perfect vibe for this art-gallery bistro.

The drinks are equally as intriguing with modern takes on vintage cocktails, with bitters and shrubs all coming from the passionate mind of Matt Pfohl.

Gnocchi with Gorgonzola Cream

(SERVES 5)

For the gnocchi:

3 tablespoons salt

4 large potatoes

1 cup all-purpose flour

3 large egg yolks

1 tablespoon butter

For the gorgonzola cream:

3 cups heavy whipping cream

2 cups gorgonzola

Special equipment:

iSi whipping cream maker

To prepare gnocchi: Dust salt on one half of a sheet pan. Poke holes on one side of each potato and place each potato holes down on the salted half sheet. Put potatoes in the oven at 400°F for about 30–45 minutes. Allow potatoes to cool, then slice the side of the potato that has the holes and scoop out the meat with a spoon. With the potato ricer rice the potatoes into a large bowl. Form a well in the center of the potatoes. Add the flour into the well, then place the egg yolks in the well and stir with your fingers.

Knead the dough lightly just until the ingredients are mixed and the dough comes together. Lay the dough on the table and allow it to rest for 5–10 minutes. Roll dough out and cut out gnocchi with a bench knife to thumb-width thickness. Place gnocchi on a flour-dusted half sheet pan.

In a large pasta pot, bring salted water to a boil. Heat up a sauté pan while you wait for the water to come to a boil. Once the water is boiling, drop in the gnocchi in batches. When the gnocchi floats to the top, remove them with a slotted spoon.

In the heated sauté pan, add 1 tablespoon butter and allow it to brown until it gives off a nutty aroma. Add the gnocchi to the brown butter and cook to a golden color. Remove the gnocchi from the pan and enjoy with the gorgonzola cream sauce.

To prepare gorgonzola cream: In a saucepan bring the heavy cream to a simmer. Slowly incorporate the gorgonzola by crumbling and folding it into the cream. Once all the cheese has melted and the mixture is smooth, add to the iSi whipping cream maker to the designated amount. Insert the nitrous oxide charger and shake. Apply the desired amount of foam on top of the gnocchi.

Note: You may serve gnocchi with your favorite pasta sauce, pesto, or cream sauce if you choose not to make the gorgonzola cream.

FLOURLESS CHOCOLATE CAKE

(SERVES 15)

1½ cups (3 sticks) unsalted butter, plus 1 tablespoon
1½ pounds semisweet chocolate chips
15 large eggs
3 cups sugar
1 tablespoon vanilla extract

Spray a 13 x 18-inch half sheet pan with nonstick vegetable spray and line with parchment paper. Spread butter on the parchment paper evenly (about 1 tablespoon butter will do the trick) and set aside.

Bring a pot of water to a boil. Dice the butter into small cubes. In a large mixing bowl, add the chocolate chips and diced butter, then place the mixing bowl above the boiling water, creating a double boiler. Mix the chocolate and butter occasionally until melted and silky smooth.

Preheat oven to 350°F. In a mixer add the eggs, sugar, and vanilla extract. Using the whisk attachment, mix until all the sugar has dissolved and the mixture is silky smooth. Slowly add the chocolate and butter mixture to the egg mixture while the mixer is still running.

Once the chocolate and egg mixture is fully incorporated, pour it onto the buttered sheet pan. Place the chocolate cake in the oven and bake for 30–45 minutes or until you can stick a toothpick into the cake and it comes out clean. Remove the cake and allow to cool.

To serve, reheat in oven to desired heat and serve with ice cream and fresh berries.

Park Cafe

604 East 1300 South
Salt Lake City, Utah 84105
(801) 487-1670
THEPARKCAFESLC.COM
Sean Miller, Chef/Owner

Seeing the line wind out the door and into the parking lot at the Park Cafe, onlookers would agree that locals know breakfast rules the day. On any given day droves of egg-craving breakfast hunters fill the booths and patio of the Park Cafe. Waiters cheerfully walk around making sure everyone has a full cup of coffee, and the kitchen is nearly bursting at the seams with short-order cooks preparing breakfast. Folks come hungry and leave happy, and it's as simple as that.

The Park Cafe is owned and run by a young couple whose personalities adorn the place, from the local band posters hanging on the walls to the quirky, sticker-covered syrup dispensers. The two have a cheerful demeanor that is obviously contagious to the whole staff. Locals who have been visiting the Park Cafe for years see the same friendly faces every time they dine.

The Park's location couldn't be any better. Before or after breakfast, you can take a walk in Liberty Park, Salt Lake's largest downtown park, through the tall, old oak trees and past fountains and Ferris wheels. Keep your eyes open for flamingos and birds of every variety at Tracy Aviary or enjoy the wild geese and ducks that flock to the park every year. You can rent a paddleboat while you visit in the summer months or sled down the main hill during the winter.

What should you eat at the Park Cafe? Well, the menu is a fairly routine greasy spoon display, but each dish is prepared with care. The Michigan Hash is a favorite around town, a mixture of hash browns, onions, peppers, mushrooms, sausage, and cheese topped with eggs made to your liking and served with a side of toast. Buttermilk or whole-grain pancakes the size of your head and french toast so thick you'll think you're in Texas satisfy those looking for something sweet.

Locals love Park Cafe, and while the food definitely stands on its own, the cafe vibe is definitely something special.

Michigan Hash

(SERVES 2)

1 large russet potato
4 links breakfast sausage
2 tablespoons vegetable oil
½ green bell pepper, chopped
¼ yellow onion, chopped
½ cup chopped mushrooms
4 eggs
⅓ cup grated cheddar cheese
Salt and pepper

Wash the potato then slice into 1-inch slices. Steam the potato slices until soft but not mushy (about 15–20 minutes). Allow the potatoes to cool, and then slice them into smaller pieces.

Brown sausage links in a skillet over medium heat. After sausage is fully cooked, allow to cool and dice into smaller pieces.

Add potatoes to the skillet and 1 tablespoon of the oil (being careful as the skillet is hot). Cook the potatoes until browned, mashing them slightly. Let cook without stirring for about 2–3 minutes then flip and cook 2 more minutes. When potatoes start to get crispy, add in the chopped bell pepper, onion, and mushrooms. Add another tablespoon of oil if needed. Cook just until onions become transparent, then add in sausage.

In a separate sauté pan, cook eggs to your preference—scrambled, fried, or poached. Divide the hash onto two plates, then top with grated cheese and cooked eggs. Salt and pepper to taste.

PENNY ANNE'S CAFE

1810 SOUTH MAIN STREET
SALT LAKE CITY, UTAH 84115
(801) 935-4760
PENNYANNSCAFE.COM
WARREN WILLEY, HEAD CHEF

We walked up to Penny Ann's unassuming cafe in the bottom of an apartment building, and our senses were instantly overcome by the smell of onions sautéing in the kitchen. Pork chile verde was being prepped for the following day, and the onions would be the base. Everything is cooked from scratch at Penny Ann's, from the boiled corned beef to the roasted turkey, the fluffy pancakes, and the pies . . . oh, the pies!

Asking the family behind Penny Ann's who is in charge of what in the restaurant may as well be a trick question. Everyone pitches in; there are no formal titles or definitions except that Warren is the head chef. It's evident that they all have distinct talents, whether in hospitality, cooking, or marketing. Each of them also overlaps with each other's strengths at times. Though Penny, one of the daughters and the cafe's namesake, may serve during business hours, she's testing pie recipes and making cakes on the side. Cindy has visions of making homemade bread soon, and Paul helps out in the kitchen and wherever else he's needed.

Originally from upstate New York, the family grew up around good food. "Mom and Dad would take us out to eat a lot . . . we would get all dressed up to go out for a nice meal." At the age of nine, Paul can remember eating liver and onions, and Warren recalls steak and lobster.

The two brothers started cooking together right out of high school, and then Warren went to culinary school. The sisters got married and moved to Utah, and the rest of the family wasn't far behind. Naturally, once they all got settled, a restaurant was in the plans. Penny Ann's opened its doors in June 2011, and now they have hopes for a second location.

Though the current location may seem a bit distracting, the food makes up for whatever is lacking in decor. But the real reason people keep coming back is that this family makes you feel like you're family when you're here. "We are grateful for everyone who comes in," says Cindy, "they are not our customers but our guests."

Peanut Butter Pie

(SERVES 8)

For the peanut butter filling:

4 ounces cream cheese, softened
⅓ cup granulated sugar
⅔ cup peanut butter
1 tablespoon butter, melted
2 teaspoons vanilla extract
⅓ cup heavy cream

For the chocolate topping:

8 ounces (about 1 cup) semisweet chocolate chips
8 ounces (1 cup) heavy cream
¼ cup chopped peanuts

For the crust:

1 graham cracker crust

To prepare peanut butter filling: Whip cream cheese, sugar, peanut butter, butter, and vanilla together until smooth, then slowly add the heavy cream and whip on high until fluffy. When finished, put into a graham cracker pie shell and spread evenly (filling should reach three-quarters of the way to the top). Refrigerate for 2 hours, then make the chocolate topping.

To prepare chocolate topping: In a small saucepan on low heat, combine the chocolate and cream and heat until all chocolate is melted. Pour chocolate topping over the peanut butter filling and top with chopped peanuts. Refrigerate until chocolate is set.

Note: If using a store-bought graham cracker crust, the slightly larger size is recommended.

Pig and a Jelly Jar

401 East 900 South
Salt Lake City, Utah 84111
(385) 202-7366
PIGANDAJELLYJAR.COM
Amy Britt, Chef/Owner

Someone once said, "Expect problems and eat them for breakfast." Well this is exactly what Amy Britt did after a portion of her beloved restaurant caught fire and forced a temporary closure. She persevered through all the chaos of insurance and remodeling for three months until she could reopen her doors. Now, on the other side, she says the fire was the best thing that could have happened to her little breakfast joint. Her team came together and are now more than ever focusing on what really matters, joyfully serving their guests.

Pig and a Jelly Jar got its name from the custom-made sausages and homemade jams that are sprinkled throughout the menu. Their menu isn't entirely local or perfectly sustainable, but they try to be as conscientious as they can about where their food comes from. Some of the sausages come from Salt Lake City's favorite butcher, Frody Volgger at Caputo's, and others come from Pennsylvania, where the pigs actually listen to music and get to roam outside. Their coffee is roasted locally by Charming Beard Coffee, and their tea is sourced from their neighbors, Tea Grotto. Pickles are made in-house, and greens are picked at a local farm.

Despite the closure because of the fire, diners remain loyal to the restaurant and their favorites on the menu. The chicken and waffles are a good bet, with a house seasoning blend, fried boneless breast, and premium maple syrup, all atop a grand waffle. Pork belly Benedict and the pig breakfast with custom-made sausage are also solid choices, but there's not much that doesn't sound appealing on their menu. Plates are served with jars of jam for you to smear over your toast or waffle, with flavors that are anything but ordinary.

Amy has a drive to bring something unique to the breakfast scene in Salt Lake, and this dedication and enthusiasm keep her restaurant alive.

BLUEBERRY LAVENDER JAM

(MAKES 4 HALF-PINT JARS)

1 bag frozen blueberries
2 cups sugar
¾ cup orange juice
2 tablespoons vanilla extract
3 tablespoons dried lavender
3 tablespoons pectin

In a pot combine blueberries, sugar, orange juice, and vanilla. Place the lavender in a cheesecloth or tea bag, then add to the blueberry mixture. Bring to a simmer and let steep for 20 minutes. Remove lavender bag and add pectin. Puree with an immersion blender or in a blender, then simmer again for 5 minutes. Remove from heat and cool. Store in jars in the refrigerator.

Serve on toast or over waffles.

RED IGUANA

736 WEST NORTH TEMPLE
SALT LAKE CITY, UTAH 84116
(801) 322-1489
REDIGUANA.COM
LUCY CARDENAS, CHEF/OWNER

An eighteen-seat Mexican diner started by the Cardenas family has became one of Salt Lake's most beloved institutions. Now enthusiastic customers wait patiently in line for the treasured Mexican cuisine that feeds over seven hundred people a day. People are loyal to Red Iguana, coming week after week, and often ordering the same dish every visit. Bill comments, "I bet 70 percent of our clientele get the same meal when they come in. It's hard to veer to something new when you find a favorite."

Lucy Cardenas, daughter of the original owners, along with her husband, Bill Coker, now run Red Iguana. They are most proud of the restaurant becoming a home for so many. Familiar faces and favorite foods make everything worthwhile. Even Lucy has her favorite: gringas with tender carne *adovada*, grilled with pineapple and peppers and served in flour tortillas.

Lucy and Bill met at a restaurant in California, following in her parents' footsteps, as they had also fallen in love over a meal. Lucy's mother, Maria Cardenas, was the one who so passionately created what is known as "Killer Mexican Food" in Salt Lake City. She brought the classics from Chihuahua and was known for her creativity. Lucy recalls, "My god-father once asked Mom to make him something delicious." She then came up with a mole, and he had a dinner that night that would live on in his memory and yet could never be re-created.

Red Iguana is known for its moles. While many restaurants offer one, maybe two, moles on their menu, Red Iguana offers eight, plus seasonal specials. A mole is a creamy-textured sauce or, more accurately, some type of creative concoction with many ingredients such as chiles, dried fruit, nuts, and chocolate. One mole on their menu has over fifty ingredients. Lucy says, "When making mole at home you just have to be creative and use quality ingredients."

The Cardenas family continue to produce artistic Mexican dishes and serve their patrons and friends who form a line down the street.

MOLE NEGRO

(SERVES 6)

7 pasilla negro chiles

6 chile mulatto

Water to soak chiles

⅓ cup peanuts

⅓ cup roughly chopped walnuts

½ cup oil, divided in half

1 (8-inch) flour tortilla

¼ yellow onion, chopped

4 cloves garlic, minced

1 overripe banana

½ poblano chile

5 cherry tomatoes

3 whole sprigs cilantro

6 whole sprigs epazote

1 bay leaf

1 avocado leaf

½ teaspoon black peppercorns

¼ teaspoon cumin seeds

¼ coriander seeds

1 clove

¾ teaspoon dried thyme

¾ teaspoon dried marjoram

½ cinnamon stick

¼ teaspoon anise seed

1 teaspoon chicken base

¾ tablet Mexican chocolate (5 ounces of a 7-ounce tablet)

3 cups water

⅓ cup sugar

Salt to taste

6 chicken breasts

To prepare mole negro: De-stem and seed chiles and then set in hot water to soak for 20 minutes. Toast peanuts and walnuts in a dry sauté pan on medium heat for about 5 minutes or in the oven on 400°F for 3 minutes, until slightly brown and fragrant.

In a large saucepan over medium-high heat, add ¼ cup oil and the flour tortilla to toast. Remove tortilla and add the onion, garlic, banana, poblano, tomatoes, cilantro, and epazote. Sauté until onion and poblano are cooked. Add all the spices, chicken base, seeds, nuts, chocolate, and chiles (do not add salt yet). Add the 3 cups water and simmer for 10 minutes. Transfer into a blender and puree until smooth.

Add the remaining ¼ cup oil to the saucepan and increase heat to high. Pour the mole back into the saucepan, being careful to not spatter yourself with hot oil. Add the sugar and salt and let simmer for 15 minutes.

In a sauté pan over medium heat, add chicken breasts and slowly sauté for 10–15 minutes or until done. Cover chicken with mole and serve with warm tortillas.

Ruth's Diner

4160 Emigration Canyon Road
Salt Lake City, Utah 84108
(801) 582-5807
RUTHSDINER.COM
Erik Nelson, Chef/Owner

Utah tourists know to start with Ruth's Diner. Locals regularly visit Ruth's Diner. It's the place to go if you have guests in town or are just looking for a good old-fashioned meal. Located in an old trolley car up Emigration Canyon, Ruth's is all about character and home cookin'.

Restaurant aside, Ruth's life was full of story, from performing as a cabaret singer to opening up a burger joint in downtown that often fed many of the misfits in the city.

As the legend goes, Ruth bought a trolley car and moved her restaurant up the canyon after the city demolished her burger joint downtown. From there the diner turned into a landmark for dining, with droves of people coming in for comfort breakfast foods or barbecue and burgers at night.

Whatever time of day you come, come hungry. In the mornings, before you even have a second to browse the menu, fluffy mile-high biscuits are delivered to your table, hot from the oven. On Thursday nights they open up the barbecue pit and fill plates to the brim with juicy barbecue and all the best sides. Portions are big and hearty, leaving you full and happy.

The outdoor patio is reason enough to visit, carved into the mountain with a stream swirling by, lights in the trees, and warming lamps keeping you cozy on cooler summer nights. Thursday evenings Ruth's hosts a local band so you can enjoy live music with your barbecue. Mornings on the patio are also great with a cup of hot coffee in hand.

Dishes not to miss include the pulled pork eggs Benedict, cinnamon roll french toast, chocolate malt pudding, and of course those mile-high biscuits that come free of charge at breakfast.

RUTH'S MILE-HIGH BISCUITS

(MAKES ABOUT 12 BISCUITS)

12 ounces flour (about 3 cups)
1½ teaspoons salt
1 tablespoon sugar
1½ teaspoons baking powder
6 tablespoons margarine, cut into cubes
¾ cup buttermilk
1 egg
¼ cup water

Preheat oven to 425°F. Combine flour, salt, sugar, baking powder, and margarine until crumbly. Add buttermilk and egg. And just enough water to moisten the dough. Mix just until combined.

Spread out dough onto a floured cutting board, about 1–1½ inches thick. Cut out biscuits with a 2-inch biscuit cutter. Place biscuits onto a cookie sheet. Bake for about 12 minutes or until golden brown.

SAFFRON VALLEY

26 E Street
Salt Lake City, Utah 84103
(801) 203-3325
SAFFRONVALLEY.COM
Lavanya Mahate, Owner
Loganathan Kannan, Chef

When you meet the team behind Saffron Valley, you just assume they are family. Chef Loganathan Kannan says, "This is not a business about making money, this is like our family. We love to cook and we love to serve." This way of thinking pervades every detail of the food and service at Saffron Valley.

Saffron began with the duo Chef Kannan and Lavanya Mahate. Lavanya previously worked at the chamber of commerce helping women around the city start businesses. Inspired by their stories, she began a business of her own. She initially started an Indian spice line, which continues today. Then, upon meeting Kannan and finding out they were from the same city in India, they decided to team up to serve their favorite Indian foods to Salt Lake residents.

The food at Saffron is a mixture of all the orients of India. So while you'll find some dishes connecting to Kannan's southern Indian roots where his grandfather and father were chefs, the menu is also filled with the best dishes from all around the country. And to keep things interesting, they hold festivals every three months at the restaurant, celebrating foods and traditions of India.

While Saffron does traditional Indian food exceptionally well, Kannan will want you to branch out a little from the typical dishes when you order. The chicken *makhni* curry dish is similar to tikka masala but with a creamier taste. The lamb Karaikudi with wintry spices is the perfect snow-day comfort food. Or try something representative of Kannan's southern Indian roots, like his *dosas*: savory lentil and rice crepes with your choice of filling, from a *panir* vegetable medley to chicken tikka. *Dahi* poppers, served with yogurt sauce and tangy chutneys, help start the meal off with cool flavor. If you want a little taste of all the meat kabobs, try the Saffron mixed platter, with several kinds of tandoor-grilled meats and cheese. To end a perfect meal at Saffron, split a mango *lassi*, a creamy fusion of yogurt and sweet mango, a taste as sweet as the family serving your meal.

CHICKEN TIKKA MASALA

(SERVES 4)

1 pound boneless, skinless chicken breast

For the marinade:

1 cup plain yogurt
3 tablespoons ginger-garlic paste (find at Indian grocer)
1 teaspoon salt
½ teaspoon freshly ground black pepper

For the sauce:

3 tablespoons butter
2 tablespoons ginger-garlic paste
2 serrano peppers, minced
2 tablespoons tomato paste
1 teaspoon garam masala
2 teaspoons paprika
8 Roma tomatoes, diced
1½ teaspoons salt
1–2 cups water
1 tablespoon dried fenugreek leaves (optional)
½ cup heavy cream
Minced fresh cilantro, for garnish

To prepare the marinade: In a large bowl, mix together yogurt, ginger-garlic paste, salt, and pepper. Add the chicken and toss to coat. Marinate at least 30 minutes, or in the refrigerator overnight.

Preheat oven to 400°F. Place the chicken in an oiled grill pan and bake for 30 minutes. Turn off the oven and let the chicken rest until the sauce is ready.

To prepare the sauce: Place a large skillet over medium heat and add the butter. When the butter has melted, add the ginger-garlic paste and serrano peppers. Sauté until lightly browned. Add the tomato paste and cook for about 3 minutes. Add the garam masala and the paprika and sauté for about 1 minute.

Add the diced tomatoes, salt, and 1 cup water. Bring to a boil, simmer, and cook until thickened, about 20 minutes. Add more water depending on how much liquid the tomatoes give.

Pour the sauce into a blender or food processor, or use an immersion blender, and process until smooth. Pour back into the skillet and bring up to a boil.

Dice the cooked chicken into bite-sized pieces. Add the chicken and fenugreek leaves, if using, to the sauce. Simmer and cook for about 10 minutes. Add the cream and stir through. Garnish with finely chopped fresh cilantro and serve over rice, with naan, or wrapped in Dosa (see recipe on next page).

DOSA

(MAKES 2 DOZEN)

For the dosa batter:

1 cup whole skinless urad dal (black gram or lentil with
black skins removed)
3 cups idli rice
1 tablespoon salt

For the dosas:

4 cups fermented dosa batter
1–1½ cups water
4 tablespoons vegetable oil

To prepare the dosa batter: Soak the dal and rice together submerged in water for 3 hours. In a blender grind the soaked rice and lentils in two batches, adding just enough water to make a smooth consistency. Combine with salt and let the batter ferment in a large bowl, lightly covered, for about 6–8 hours in a warm place.

To prepare dosas: Add enough water to the fermented batter so you have a smooth, pouring consistency. Make sure the batter is not too watery; it should coat the back of a spoon.

Heat an iron griddle and grease lightly with oil. Pour about ½ cup batter in the center of the griddle, using a round ladle. With the back of the ladle, gently spread the batter in a circular motion from the center toward the sides of the griddle, forming an 8–10-inch concentric circle.

Drizzle about 1 teaspoon oil around the edges of the dosa and drizzle a few drops on the top as well. If the griddle is greased adequately and is not sticky, the edge of the dosa will start to come off the pan in about 1 minute or so. Use a spatula to gently lift the dosa and turn over. Cook this side for about 1 minute.

Place a few tablespoons of Chicken Tikka Masala as filling in the dosa and fold into a semicircle. Serve hot.

Mango Lassi

(MAKES ABOUT 2 CUPS)

1 cup chopped mango (peeled and stone removed)
   or ¾ cup mango puree
1 cup plain yogurt
½ cup milk
4 teaspoons sugar
Dash of yellow food coloring (optional)

Put mango, yogurt, milk, sugar, and food coloring into a blender and blend for 2 minutes, then pour into individual glasses and serve chilled. The lassi can be kept refrigerated for up to 48 hours.

Sage's Cafe

234 West 900 South
Salt Lake City, Utah 84101
(801) 322-3790
sagescafe.com
Ian Brandt, Chef/Owner

You have to be a scientist of sorts when you cook for vegans and vegetarians. This crowd is cooking a lot at home, experimenting with flavors and unusual combinations, so when they go out to eat, they want something even more interesting than what they create in their own kitchens. Luckily, Ian Brandt provides just that, always researching and experimenting to come up with creations all his own. Local, organic, and unprocessed are a high priority whenever possible at Sage's Cafe.

As a kid Ian had a curious palate, even trying escargot and other foods kids usually avoid. His curiosity continues today as he takes on the challenge to satisfy the vegan and vegetarian crowds in Salt Lake. Not just anyone could do what Ian does. He's a scientist in his own right, turning things like shiitake mushrooms into a flavorful "escargot," and creaming carrots into a sweet form of vegetarian pâté.

Sage's Cafe has a cult following. Pizza night every Tuesday and Meatless Monday brings in folks from all walks. And those who've been dining here for years didn't skip a beat when the cafe's location changed.

The new spot provides a second dining area, the Jade Room, appropriately named after the building's previous Asian diner, the Jade Cafe. This redesigned, midcentury-styled room is available for private parties and late night small plates and drinks, alcoholic and nonalcoholic. Pass around the mushroom escargot as you catch up with friends or listen to a band play.

Ian's ideas and philosophies are helping boost the growing vegetarian/vegan scene as more and more vegan, raw, and vegetarian cafes are opening up around town. And with more options more people, vegetarian or not, are seeing how flavorful vegetarian dining can be.

SAGE'S SHIITAKE ESCARGOT WITH CARROT BUTTER PÂTÉ

(SERVES 8–10 AS AN APPETIZER)

For the carrot butter pâté:

1¼ pounds carrots, peeled and coined

¾ cup macadamia nuts

½ cup safflower or canola oil

2 tablespoons maple syrup

½ tablespoon vanilla extract

½ tablespoon salt

For the shiitake escargot:

1¼ cups water

¼ cup balsamic vinegar

½ cup red cooking wine

¼ cup minced garlic

¼ cup extra-virgin olive oil

2 teaspoons ground rosemary

2 teaspoons ground mustard

1½ tablespoons sea salt

8 ounces, by weight, fresh shiitake mushrooms

To prepare carrot butter pâté: Boil carrots in 1½ gallons of water for 2 hours. Strain carrots and save stock for a wide variety of other recipes.

In a blender combine carrots, nuts, oil, maple syrup, vanilla, and salt and blend until a velvet puree. Set aside.

Note: You can use this carrot butter as a pâté for topping baguette slices, as a stuffing for french toast, and as a sauce or soup base.

To prepare shiitake escargot: In a blender, combine all marinade ingredients. Slice the shiitake mushrooms vertically, keeping the stem and the mushroom intact. Soak the shiitake mushrooms in the marinade overnight.

Heat oven to broil or at the highest temperature. Place mushrooms and a little leftover marinade into a 2-inch-deep roasting pan. The mushrooms should not be layered deeper than two mushroom slices. You can either make multiple small pans or one large pan of roasted mushrooms.

Portion 2 cups of the carrot butter into a soufflé dish or stainless baking pan. Broil both the mushrooms and carrot butter for approximately 8–12 minutes.

Serve with toasted baguette slices. You will need about thirty-two crostinis to match the amount of this appetizer.

If you are preparing this appetizer for only two people, reduce the recipe or just portion out less of the marinated mushroom and carrot butter to roast. You can keep the mushrooms and pâté in your refrigerator for 5 days and enjoy this wonderful appetizer with a glass of red wine each day in the early evening!

Wine Pairing: This is one of a few dishes that will match perfectly with a rich red wine. Ian suggests Parallel Vineyards' Cabernet Sauvignon.

Tea Pairing: Choose the rich Pu-erh Organic Wild Tree Mini-Tuo Cha from Rishi Teas, which will match the rich flavors of the escargot.

Solitude Mountain Resort

12000 Big Cottonwood Road
Solitude, Utah 84121
(801) 534-1400
SKISOLITUDE.COM
Scott Deseelhorst, Owner
Jean Louis Montecot, Chef
Greg Neville, Food and Beverage

The Deseelhorst family migrated north from Arizona to operate their beloved Solitude Mountain Resort. The ski area was started in the 1950s; in 1977, Gary Deseelhorst, along with a few other investors, picked up Solitude Mountain Resort, which at the time was little more than a few ski lifts and an outhouse. The Deseelhorst family planned on elevating the ski resort from small and humble to large and somehow still humble.

Almost forty years later the Solitude land in Big Cottonwood Canyon bears witness to the family's vision of a village with multiple restaurants, lifts, and excuses to spend an afternoon, evening, or weekend on the slopes and in their dining rooms. Through the course of the last few decades, Solitude slowly made their development (the only one allowed in the canyon) into a place locals love and travelers can find first-class service at a local's pace.

Recently Solitude acquired Greg Neville (founder of Lugano) to manage the dining scene around Solitude and push it to the next level. On any given winter's evening, you'll find St. Bernards, the Yurt, Library Bar, and Honeycomb Grill packed with skiers looking to refuel. Greg is quick to recognize that these restaurants do really well at serving the guests in the village. At the same time he believes the next step for Solitude dining is one that calls the Salt Lake City foodie up the canyon simply for the food, sans skis.

If you're looking for a completely different dining experience than you'll get anywhere else in the city, make reservations at the Yurt. To get to the Yurt, you must strap on snowshoes and work your way through the dark woods for an evening of great beverages and a prefixed menu. It's wintry, quiet, homey, and beyond warm in every sense of the word.

POUTINE

(SERVES 4)

1 ounce dried porcini mushrooms (rehydrated with 4 ounces red wine and 1 whole clove garlic)

2 tablespoons butter

2 tablespoons flour

2 cups mushroom stock

Salt

Freshly ground black pepper

2 pounds Idaho white potatoes

Oil for frying

½ pound fresh gruyère cheese, shredded

To prepare mushroom gravy: In a saucepan over medium heat, combine the minced porcini mushrooms, butter, and flour. Stir until incorporated. Cook for 12–15 minutes for a dark roux. Stir in the stock and the juice from the porcini mushrooms. Season with salt and pepper. Bring to a boil, then reduce the heat to medium low and continue cooking for 15–20 minutes. Remove from the heat and keep warm (the gravy should stick to the back of a spoon).

To prepare french fries: Peel the potatoes and cut into fries, 4 inches by ½ inch. Bring a pot of salted water to a boil. Add the potatoes to the boiling water and blanch for 4 minutes. Remove, drain, and cool completely. Heat 3–4 inches of oil to 325°F in a heavy-bottomed skillet and fry the potatoes for 5–6 minutes, turning occasionally, until golden brown. Remove fries from oil and drain on paper towels. Season with salt and pepper.

To serve: Increase oven temperature to 400°F. Mound the fries into individual 16-ounce bowls. Spoon the mushroom gravy over the fries. Top with gruyère cheese. Bake for 5 minutes, until cheese is melted, and serve.

Utah Steelhead Trout Tartare

(SERVES 4)

6 ounces Utah steelhead trout, finely diced but not
   minced and chilled

2 ounces extra-virgin olive oil

2 ounces minced shallots

½ ounce diced chives

Juice from ½ Meyer lemon

Salt and pepper to taste

Deep-fried sunchokes (see recipe)

For the deep-fried sunchokes:

3 sunchokes, finely sliced

Oil for frying

Sea salt

2 ounces crème fraîche

1 ounce chive oil

In a bowl add trout, olive oil, shallots, chives, lemon juice, salt, and pepper and gently fold together. Taste seasoning for appropriate amounts of lemon, salt, and pepper and adjust as needed. Spoon tartare mixture into desired ring mold on a plate. Top with fried sunchoke chips. Garnish with crème fraîche and chive oil. Enjoy!

To prepare sunchokes: Slice sunchokes into thin rounds (about 1/16 inch thick); immediately drop the slices into a bowl of ice water to prevent browning. Rinse and drain then pat dry with paper towels. Pour enough oil into a large deep skillet to reach a depth of ½ inch. Heat oil to 375°F. Working in batches, fry sunchoke slices until golden brown, stirring occasionally, 3 to 4 minutes. Using a skimmer, transfer chips to paper towels to drain. Season with sea salt.

TAQUERIA 27

1615 SOUTH FOOTHILL DRIVE
SALT LAKE CITY, UTAH 84108
(385) 259-0712
TAQUERIA27.COM
TODD GARDINER, CHEF/OWNER

Tacos and tequila put Taqueria 27 on the map. You'll find this taqueria on your way up to the mountains or as you're heading toward downtown and the university. It's easy to miss from the street but too memorable to forget once you've visited. These are not your traditional tacos and margaritas but a whole new wave of sophistication for these Mexican favorites.

The chef, Todd Gardiner, chose a style of food for the way it lent itself to his creativity. After years of working at other local restaurants, he knew exactly what he wanted when he opened up his own spot: a menu that could evolve, with plenty of opportunity for inspiration.

As a few examples of his innovative spirit, fried chicken tacos with mint salsa and Sriracha are a weekly special, PBLTA tacos (Pork Belly Lettuce Tomato Avocado) are a regular menu item, and wild mushroom tacos are a unique favorite for meat eaters and vegetarians alike. If you're really going out on a limb, the pear and beet taco with balsamic and blue cheese is a real treasure.

The menu also offers six varieties of guacamole, from traditional guac to spicy mango. The guac of the day helps keep things fresh. You'd never think to put green apple, pickled red onion, and Serrano peppers in your guac, but you'll be glad Todd thought of it.

Flavors of every component of the menu stand out. Even the corn tortillas are made fresh in-house. The ingredients are so fresh at Taqueria 27 that they don't even own a freezer. And if you're into tequila, the selection is vast. As Todd says, "Meals at Taqueria are best shared, family style, so you can try more on the menu." And everyone in the family will find something to enjoy.

PBLTA Tacos

(MAKES 8 TACOS, SERVES 2–4)

For the tacos:

8 pieces pork belly (about 1 pound)

8 corn or flour tortillas

3 tablespoons jalapeño aioli (see recipe)

½ cup shredded lettuce

8 slices ripe avocado

8 slices ripe tomato

For the jalapeño aioli:

1½ cups mayonnaise

2 tablespoons red wine vinegar

2 teaspoons salsa chile morita or chipotle puree

½ ounce raw jalapeño

¼ ounce cilantro

2 tablespoons fresh lime juice

¼ tablespoon chili powder

½ teaspoon black pepper

To prepare tacos: Sear both sides of the pork belly on a cast-iron griddle over medium-high heat. While the belly is cooking, warm the tortillas and lay flat to build the tacos. Slice the pork belly into eight even slices. Begin by spreading some jalapeño aioli on the tortillas, then add lettuce, avocado, and tomato and top with one piece of pork belly per taco. Fold tacos and serve.

To prepare jalapeño aioli: Place all ingredients in a bowl and mix well using an immersion blender, or whisk by hand.

THE ROSE ESTABLISHMENT

235 SOUTH 400 WEST
SALT LAKE CITY, UTAH 84101
(801) 990-6270
THEROSEESTB.COM
ERICA O'BRIEN, OWNER

When The Rose Establishment opened, there was a noticeable gasp of excitement in Salt Lake City. It was almost a stamp of legitimacy for the shop's intention and design. With its success The Rose gave a green light for other restaurateurs and food entrepreneurs who were skeptical to invest as much money in their environment as they do in their food and beverage. Prior to this, Salt Lake had experienced relatively few eateries and shops that made the same statement (and risk) for design.

Exposed wood, weathered metals, storied found objects, and a lack of Wi-Fi invite you into a beautiful analog world of reading or talking or looking out a window. Owner Erica O'Brien made a risky decision to keep her place Wi-Fi-free at a time when coffee

shop–goers might consider withholding Wi-Fi as a sin punishable by death. After all, what good is a coffee shop if not to sit anonymously and work for hours and hours after purchasing only one cup of coffee? To Erica it's a place of community and connection uninhibited by noses buried in computer screens, endlessly browsing Facebook.

Even if the environment wasn't near-perfect and wonderfully warm with its rustic table and clean countertops, the menu would bring you back. For one, they serve San Francisco legend Four Barrel Coffee on French press, pour over, and espresso along with a small offering of local Charming Beard Coffee Roasters for pour over. Perhaps at the foundation of The Rose, it was a coffee-forward shop. As it ages, the menu deepens with toasts, mueslis, soups, salads, sandwiches, and pastries, all that match the brand of the room perfectly—tactile and intentional.

The Rose Establishment certainly wasn't SLC's first coffee shop or cafe, but somehow after just a few short years, it's hard to imagine northwest downtown without it.

THE ROSE SHORTBREAD

(MAKES 2 DOZEN)

For the shortbread:

½ cup powdered sugar
2½ cups unbleached pastry flour
1¼ cups (2½ sticks) unsalted butter
¾ teaspoon salt

For the glaze:

½ tablespoon rose and hibiscus tea (1 tea bag)
¼ cup water
¼ teaspoon lemon juice
2¼ cups powdered sugar
Rose petals, for garnish

To prepare shortbread: Sift powdered sugar and set aside. Sift flour and set aside.

Bring the butter to just over room temperature in the microwave; it should be soft but not melted. Cream the butter and salt in a stand mixer. Scrape down the bowl and add the powdered sugar. Cream until light and fluffy, about 1 minute on medium speed.

Scrape down the bowl and add the flour. Mix on low speed until incorporated, scrape the bowl again, and mix on medium speed until well combined.

Wrap the dough in plastic and let sit at room temperature for 30 minutes.

Roll the dough to between ¼ and ½ inch depending on preference. Cut with a circle or any shape cookie cutter, then transfer to a sheet pan lined with parchment paper, placing cookies at least 1 inch apart from each other.

Let chill in refrigerator for at least 1 hour and up to 24 hours.

Preheat oven to 325°F. Bake shortbread for 12–15 minutes depending on thickness. While cooling, prepare glaze.

To prepare glaze: Steep the tea in ¼ cup boiling water for 10 minutes. Strain the tea, then add lemon juice to the tea. Whisk in powdered sugar until desired glazing consistency.

Glaze the cookies with a pastry brush in a circular motion (you can also use the back of a spoon). Finish with three small rose petals in the middle of the cookie.

LIBERTY PARK

In 1881 Salt Lake City purchased a plot of land from Brigham Young that would eventually anchor and identify a neighborhood. The city planned to introduce and dedicate the newly purchased public land on July 4, 1881, only to postpone it out of respect for President Garfield, who was assassinated days prior on July 2.

Over the last century Liberty Park has housed a zoo, a carnival, and a handful of other uses incongruent with the original vision of the urban haven. A few decades ago a managing group of the park voted to phase out all the uses that didn't work well with a public-use space (e.g., carnival) and turn up the volume on the open green spaces and playgrounds.

Today you'll find the 80-acre park alive with the tenants of the almost-gentrified Liberty Wells neighborhood made strong by Liberty Park, the Park Cafe, and the nearby 9th and 9th neighborhood housing some of the establishments awakening the downtown scene—Pago, Zuriick, Apartment 202, Liberty Tap House, and more.

Farro with Roasted Cauliflower, Caramelized Shallot, and Feta

(SERVES 4 AS A SIDE OR 2 AS A MEAL)

For the farro:

2 teaspoons oil

1 shallot, thinly sliced

2 teaspoons salt

2 cups farro

Few sprigs of fresh thyme

1 small head cauliflower (or ½ of a large one)

2 teaspoons cumin

1 small carrot, grated

¼ cup roasted pistachios

Pepper to taste

¼ cup crumbled feta

For the garlic vinaigrette:

2 cloves garlic

¼ cup white wine vinegar (or any tasty vinegar you like)

1 tablespoon Dijon mustard

2 tablespoons roughly chopped fresh parsley

1 teaspoon salt

2 teaspoons maple syrup or honey

¾ cup extra-virgin olive oil

To prepare farro: In a medium pot heat 1 teaspoon oil on medium-high heat, then add the shallot and ½ teaspoon of the salt. Stirring occasionally, cook shallot until golden and soft, about 5 minutes. Remove shallot from the pan and reserve for later. Return the pot to medium-high heat and add farro, remaining 1½ teaspoons salt, and thyme. Toast farro for about 30 seconds, stirring constantly. Add 6 cups water and bring to a boil, then reduce heat to a simmer and let farro cook for about 20 minutes, stirring occasionally. Drain excess water and let cool.

Meanwhile, preheat oven to 350°F. Chop cauliflower into bite-sized pieces and spread on a baking sheet. Add cumin and remaining 1 teaspoon oil and mix. Roast cauliflower in the oven for about 5–7 minutes, until golden and fragrant.

In a large mixing bowl, add farro, cauliflower, shallot, carrot, pistachios, and 1 cup vinaigrette and mix well. Season to taste with salt and pepper. To serve, divide among bowls and top evenly with feta.

To prepare garlic vinaigrette: Combine all ingredients except oil in a food processor and puree. With the machine still running, slowly add the oil. Taste for seasoning. This will make a little more than what you need, but the extra will keep in the refrigerator for a week.

TIN ANGEL

365 WEST 400 SOUTH
SALT LAKE CITY, UTAH 84101
(801) 328-4155
THETINANGEL.COM
JERRY LIEDTKE, CHEF/OWNER

Tears come to Jerry's eyes as he speaks of his father's care for those marginalized in the city and of his unique space in the Salt Lake dining scene. Jerry Liedtke, owner of Tin Angel, simply can't help but be warm and welcoming given his family line. His father owned a bar named The Tin Angel on 400 South in the 1960s, which, after a series of events, opened its doors to the drag queen population of Salt Lake City. Today Jerry opens the doors to those looking for an approachable style to fine dining, what he termed "punk rock fine dining," and gives his high-end clientele a view of the city that cannot be ignored given that the restaurant stands right beside a well-known hangout for the homeless population of Salt Lake.

Jerry, along with his wife, Kestrel, and friend Robin, opened Tin Angel. After spending many years in the kitchens of the best independently owned restaurants in Salt Lake, he decided this wasn't just a job; cooking would be his career. He and his wife first set out to open a little cafe out of their trailer, but ended up settling back in Salt Lake when Kestrel found out she was pregnant. Salt Lake would be the destination of their business and family, a welcomed final destination, as Jerry mentions, "I always like coming home to Salt Lake after traveling."

Jerry hires an eclectic staff, giving the restaurant even more unique expression. He even gives his dishwashers a chance to create their own version of the house bread pudding, a recipe that changes seasonally and whimsically. Recipes come from thrift store books or international cooking ideas and are twisted and tried until they are perfectly their own, even naming them on the menu with more widely known terms. Jerry says, "The best cookbooks are those with recipes that read like stories . . . a dash of this or a smear of that." And he encourages his cooks to be expressive in their cooking. The menu bleeds this spirit, with dishes like gypsy pork empanada, quinoa timbal, smokey gnocchi, espresso crusted beef tenderloin, and whimsical flavors of panna cotta that change based on the season.

The house favorite soup is a mixture of spinach and fontina cheese. Jerry generously offers that the soup's secret lies within the type of cheese: "Use Swedish fontina instead of Danish, so the cheese is not as pungent and doesn't overtake the flavor of the spinach." And for the coveted bread pudding: "Make sure the bread pudding is moist before you put it in the oven, not too much liquid but just enough."

Tin Angel still breathes Jerry Sr.'s care for the city and for individuality, and those who eat here enjoy this distinction in every thoughtful bite.

Tin Angel Bread Pudding

(SERVES 6–8)

3 large eggs

½ cup sugar

1 teaspoon vanilla extract

Zest of ½ lemon or orange

2 cups heavy cream

4–6 cups torn bread (½ of it croissants)

½ cup chocolate pieces or chips

¼ cup cranberries or cherries or figs or rhubarb, strawberries, apples—whatever you find that is lovely at the farmers' market

Grease a 7 x 11-inch pan with oil or butter.

In a large bowl mix eggs, sugar, vanilla, lemon zest, and cream. Add the bread, chocolate, and cranberries.

Pour mixture into the greased pan and cover with foil. Preheat oven to 350°F. Let bread mixture rest and absorb while the oven preheats. Bake covered for 35 minutes, then uncover and bake for an additional 5 minutes.

Serve warm with caramel sauce or vanilla ice cream.

Special tips: At Tin Angel we take whole chocolate and chop it down for a variety of sizes. We also reconstitute dried fruits in the winter by soaking them in liquor for added flavor. Brandy or a sweet sherry work great, but we have also been known to use whiskey.

TIN ANGEL'S SPINACH & FONTINA ZUPPA

(SERVES 6)

4 tablespoons (½ stick) butter

½ cup flour

½ cup chopped sweet onion

Salt and pepper to taste

2 tablespoons canola oil

2 cups white wine

2 cups vegetable stock

3 cups heavy cream

1 cup cubed fontina cheese

2 cups lightly packed chopped fresh spinach

2 tablespoons lemon juice

Begin by making a roux with the butter and flour by first melting the butter in a skillet and then adding the flour slowly. Stir together for about 3 minutes, until the mixture becomes a thick paste. Set aside.

In a 6- to 8-quart saucepan, sauté the sweet onion in canola oil until it becomes translucent (do not caramelize or brown). Season the onion with salt and pepper. Deglaze the pan with white wine, using a wooden spoon to scrape any brown pieces from the pan. Add vegetable stock and cream. Bring to a simmer and then stir in the roux. Cook on low until soup starts to thicken, about 10 minutes. Add fontina cheese and keep stirring to prevent scorching. Stir until the cheese has melted, then remove from heat and let cool completely.

In a food processor blend spinach with lemon juice. After the soup has cooled completely, combine with the spinach and blend again until smooth. You can do this in the soup pot if you have an immersion blender, or pour the cool soup into the food processor with the spinach. Be sure the soup has cooled completely before adding the spinach; otherwise the spinach will brown. Mix them together when they are cool and then reheat. Season with salt and pepper to taste. At the Tin Angel we garnish with tomato oil and place a crostini on top just before serving.

TRIO

680 South 900 East
Salt Lake City, Utah 84102
(801) 533-8746
TRIODINING.COM
Jennifer West, Head Chef

Sadly, few Salt Lake City restaurants boast women head chefs. While many women have found their places in bakeries and making desserts at restaurants, women as head chefs are few and far between. So you can imagine our excitement when we met Jennifer West at Trio, a bubbly personality yet pretty hard core in the kitchen.

After culinary school at Le Cordon Bleu in Portland, Jennifer moved to Salt Lake for the skiing, as many of us did, then she just couldn't find a reason to leave. She quickly proved her worth in a restaurant at Alta Ski Resort. It was the perfect match for her to best enjoy the benefits of living in the mountains. At Alta they made everything from scratch, which meant she had to teach the young ski bums in her line how to cook well too.

Today she still gets up to Alta pretty often, though she's not risking it as much as she once did. She wears her avalanche beacon and stays in bounds these days. Being in charge of two busy city kitchens is enough to make her a bit more straight laced.

At Trio she takes pride in the fresh-made pastas and breads like their focaccia. They're doing more and more in-house as of late. "We're trying to make the food scene better around," she says about her role in the local food awakening. Trio's owner, Mikel Trapp, supports her wholeheartedly. He owns a few places around town where Jennifer's skills are put to work.

On Jennifer's arm you'll read, "Pressure makes diamonds," which has proved true in her culinary journey. Though she currently stands out in the Salt Lake chef scene, we are sure that she is grooming the way for more women to come.

Manila Clams

(SERVES 2–4)

For the braised fennel:

1 fennel bulb (sometimes called anise; 10–12 ounces) with fronds

¾ tablespoon extra-virgin olive oil

⅛ teaspoon salt

Dash of black pepper

¼ cup reduced-sodium chicken broth

⅛ cup water

1 tablespoon oil

8 ounces manila clams, rinsed under cold water

1 teaspoon salt

1 ounce braised fennel

1 teaspoon minced garlic

1 teaspoon minced shallots

1 ounce cooked bacon

¼ cup white wine

1 ounce roasted red peppers

¼ cup (½ stick) butter

2 slices grilled bread

Lemon slices

To braise fennel: Cut off and discard stalks from fennel bulb, reserving fronds. Chop 1 tablespoon fronds and discard remainder. Cut bulb lengthwise into ½-inch-thick slices, leaving core intact.

Heat oil in a skillet over moderately high heat until hot but not smoking, then brown fennel slices well, turning over once, 3–4 minutes total.

Reduce heat to low. Sprinkle fennel with salt and pepper, then add broth and water. Cook, covered, until fennel is tender, 10–12 minutes. Sprinkle with fennel fronds.

To prepare manila clams: Heat 1 tablespoon oil over medium-high heat. Once hot add the clams and season with salt. Sauté the clams for 1 minute.

Add fennel, garlic, shallots, and bacon and sauté for 1 more minute. Add white wine, roasted red peppers, and butter.

Place lid on pot and cook until clams are all open and butter is melted. Throw away any clams that did not open. Check seasoning.

Serve with warm grilled bread and lemon slices.

TULIE BAKERY

863 EAST 700 SOUTH
SALT LAKE CITY, UTAH 84102
(801) 883-9741
TULIEBAKERY.COM
LESLIE SEGGAR, BAKER/OWNER

It's no secret that Tulie Bakery is loved. On weekend mornings you may find a line out the door and no seat empty in this little neighborhood bakery. Dogs sit tied up outside and bikes lie turned on their sides, all in the name of a good pastry and a cup of coffee.

Most know what to order: the Morning Bun, a cinnamon-roll-like pastry that takes over eighteen hours to make, with layers of flakey dough and a hint of orange that is crispy and gooey all at the same time. Almond fans will find the almond croissant beyond compare. Other favorites are the chocolate bouchon, made in traditional fashion to the original bouchon from Thomas Keller's bakery; the croissant, perfectly crisp on the exterior with layer upon layer of buttery pastry; the quiche, made fresh in-house with a variety of ingredients; and the french toast, made with house-made brioche bread and topped with crème fraîche and blueberries. If you visit on the weekend, their beignets will taunt you lying next to the register.

While the pastries easily win over clientele, the story behind this little bakery is just as rich. Leslie Seggar started baking when her little boy turned ten years old. She was on the search for a special cake and couldn't find what she was looking for in town, so she ventured out to make her own. That was the first step toward owning her own bakery. This self-taught baker made a huge career shift, as she found her heart more in the kitchen than in her work as a clinical psychologist.

Today the love of baking spreads deep and wide throughout the kitchen at Tulie, and many have found it a favorable place to work. Upbeat employees, constantly surrounded by and filled with butter and sugar, create a sweet ambience.

TULIE FRENCH TOAST

(SERVES 5, 2 SLICES PER PERSON)

For the crème frâiche:

1 cup heavy cream
⅛ cup buttermilk

For the french toast:

1 thick loaf of brioche
8 eggs
½ cup whole milk
2–3 tablespoons granulated sugar
1 tablespoon vanilla extract
Dash of cinnamon

For serving:

Crème fraîche
Powdered sugar
Blueberries

To prepare crème fraîche: Combine cream and buttermilk in a crock or a container with a secure lid. Leave at room temperature until thickened (about 2 days, depending on the temperature).

To prepare french toast: Slice brioche into ten slices. Heat a large skillet or a panini press. Mix together eggs, milk, sugar, vanilla, and cinnamon. Dip bread slices into egg mixture, then transfer to the skillet or grill. Cook until golden on both sides. Repeat with remaining slices.

Serve with homemade crème fraîche, a dusting of powdered sugar, and a fistful of fresh blueberries.

VERTICAL DINER

2280 SOUTH WEST TEMPLE
SALT LAKE CITY, UTAH 84115
(801) 484-8378
VERTICALDINER.COM
IAN BRANDT, CHEF/OWNER

Hipsters unite at this South Salt Lake vegetarian diner, though it must also be noted that many outside of the fixed gear/tight jeans/tofu-eating crowd also enjoy the flavors of Vertical Diner. Leather booths and typical diner seating line the narrow cafe, along with eclectic art and funky tunes. Regulars sit in their habitual seats as the waiter brings out their favorites.

Even the waitresses love the food. One mentioned getting the job just so she could eat here more often. She also notes the house favorites are the jerk chicken, veggie burgers, and buffalo tigers, which are fried chicken tenders in spicy buffalo sauce. Of course, whenever chicken is mentioned, they really mean a chicken substitute. Proteins like tempeh, tofu, portobello mushrooms, and black beans make each dish especially hearty and filling. Desserts are a special treat here, and the Shoofly Cake is a favorite. Owner/chef Ian Brandt adapted his grandma's special recipe for a vegetarian diet, so now his favorite family dessert is shared with many.

Vertical Diner serves breakfast and lunch, but you don't have to wake up too early to enjoy breakfast foods here, as brunch is served all day and the diner doesn't even open until 10 a.m. Brunch favorites include the biscuits and gravy with tempeh bacon, The King pancakes with bananas and peanut butter, and The Mountain: hash browns, tofu scramble, sausage, peppers, and onions topped with guacamole.

As for the building Vertical resides in, legend has it that a brickyard worker saved up bricks in his lunchbox every day so he could eventually build this diner. And that's where the restaurant got its first name, the Lunch Box Cafe. From there, a couple of fishermen owned it, naming it appropriately after themselves, Chuck and Fred's, and they placed a boat on top of the structure. This quirky pair would oftentimes leave a sign on their door noting that they were "Gone Fishin." They passed the building to Jim Sorensen, who then handed it off to Ian. It's now in good hands with Ian, thriving as a wallet-friendly spot for healthy versions of greasy spoon favorites.

Vertical Diner Shoofly Cake

(SERVES 12)

For the streusel:

½ cup shortening
4 cups unbleached flour
1 teaspoon salt
1½ cups sugar

For the cake:

1½ cups water
½ cup sugar
½ cup molasses
1½ tablespoons white vinegar
1 tablespoon baking soda

In a mixing bowl use a dough blender or fork to cut chilled shortening into flour. Add salt and sugar to create a crumble.

Preheat oven to 375°F. Thoroughly grease and flour a 9 x 13-inch cake pan.

In a pot (approximately 1 gallon size), bring water, sugar, molasses, and vinegar nearly to a boil. Just as the liquid reaches a boil, turn off heat, add baking soda, and stir really well, being careful not to allow the liquid to foam over.

Pour the liquid into the bottom of the greased cake pan. Sprinkle the crumble evenly over the liquid in the cake pan, allowing some to sink and some to float. Use your fingers to press about 75 percent of the streusel below the surface. You want to see one-quarter of the dry mix floating and three-quarters of the dry mix absorbed into the liquid.

Bake the cake for approximately 1 hour or until the cake is cooked through. Check after about 35 minutes (or when you think it is done) with a toothpick. If the toothpick comes out close to dry (with a few crumbs), then the cake is done.

Serve this moist molasses cake with vegan ice cream, soak it with a shot of espresso, or enjoy it with both.

VINTO

418 EAST 200 SOUTH
SALT LAKE CITY, UTAH 84102
(801) 539-9999
VINTO.COM
AMBER BILLINGSLY, PASTRY CHEF
TRENT CAMPBELL, HEAD CHEF

If one word was used to describe Vinto, it would be savvy. Their table-side ordering system moves the night along efficiently, and they offer modern pizza topping combinations, a great price point, and an award-winning pastry chef.

The man behind all this savviness is David Harries, a longtime participant in the local food scene, owning and operating some of the best restaurants in town. He's an entrepreneur of the best sort.

At Vinto David created a system that could be enjoyed by a variety of diners—from those wanting a quick slice to those wanting to sip wine with their pizza and stay a while. With handheld ordering devices the waiters can quickly get your order to the kitchen so pizzas and pastas are out in remarkable time. As for the pizza, they create demand in Salt Lake City for old favorites done in a new way.

Those who want lighter fare, as well as those who want a little something finer than pizza, will both be satisfied. Try one of the chop salads or a hearty pasta if you're not in the pizza mood; neither will disappoint. They have their recipes dialed in, and that's just a peek at how their whole business runs.

David creates space—space for the chefs to be creative and have opportunities outside of the restaurant, and space for locals to dine comfortably and enjoyably. Trent Campbell, head chef at Vinto, finds his creative outlet in the seasonal specials, while he also continues to enjoy making the menu staples. The Patate Pizza (his favorite) is drizzled with truffle oil and topped with Yukon Gold potatoes and fontina cheese.

For desserts, Vinto found great talent in Amber Billingsly and won her over to the team. She's been at Vinto longer than any other restaurant in her career; after a few years at Vinto, she was awarded best pastry chef in the city. She now provides all the desserts, including her famous Butterscotch Budino, for both the Salt Lake and Park City locations. Her tip for making the perfect budino: "Don't multitask. The custard can scorch or curdle easily so you have to be careful."

Butterscotch Budino

(SERVES 8)

4 cups heavy cream

1 cup whole milk

1¼ cups light brown sugar

½ cup water

1 whole large egg

3 large egg yolks

5 tablespoons cornstarch

4 tablespoons (½ stick) unsalted butter, cut into small pieces

2 tablespoons dark rum (bourbon is also very good!)

1½ teaspoons fine sea salt or kosher salt

Measure cream and milk into a measuring cup or bowl and set aside.

Combine brown sugar and water in a large, heavy-bottomed saucepan over medium heat and let brown sugar mixture come to a simmer. Turn to medium-high and cook until dark (about 5 minutes), with slow rolling bubbles and poofs of fragrant smoke. Do not walk away; it goes from dark to burnt quickly!

Slowly add cream mixture. Do so carefully; the mixture will bubble furiously, and caramel burns hurt. The mixture will seize, but that's okay. Whisk occasionally until cream and sugar become one. Cook until mixture comes to a simmer. Turn off heat.

While sugar and cream are heating, whisk egg and egg yolks and cornstarch together until smooth. Pour half of the hot caramel cream into a measuring cup and very slowly add this to the egg mixture, whisking constantly. Take your time; you don't want to scramble your eggs. Pour this mixture back into the measuring cup.

Turn heat back on under remaining caramel cream, medium-high. Pour the eggy cream mixture into the saucepan, whisking constantly. Keep whisking until thick and the first bubbles pop on the surface. Immediately remove from heat and whisk in butter, rum, and salt until smooth.

Pour mixture through a sieve and into a large measuring cup or spouted bowl, pressing with a rubber spatula to get all the warm, pudding-y goodness through. Immediately portion into your prettiest parfait glasses or bowls and chill. Serve with a thin veneer of caramel sauce, a tiny sprinkle of coarse sea salt, and a dollop of unsweetened whipped cream.

Patate Pizza

(SERVES 2–4)

1 pizza dough

Drizzle of garlic oil

Pinch of chopped fresh rosemary

1 ounce garlic paste (see recipe)

1 ounce fontina cheese, shredded

1 ounce goat cheese

3 ounces sliced Yukon Gold potatoes (see cooking directions)

Pinch of salt and black pepper

½ ounce wild arugula

Drizzle of white truffle oil

To prepare garlic paste: Remove husks from the cloves of a whole garlic bulb. Place all the cloves from the bulb in a small saucepan. Add oil until it just covers the garlic. Cook on high heat until the oil is hot. Turn down the heat to low and cook until the garlic turns a golden brown color (about 30 minutes or less). Strain the oil and set aside (this will be brushed on the pizza later!). Using a food processor, puree the garlic cloves with a tablespoon of garlic oil. Puree until smooth. If the mixture is too thick, add a bit more garlic oil.

To prepare potatoes: Slice the Yukon Gold potatoes as thin as potato chips. Place the potato slices in a bowl and drizzle some olive oil over them. Add a pinch of salt and pepper to taste. Toss the potatoes until well coated. Place in the oven on an oiled cookie sheet. Bake at 500°F for about 10–12 minutes or until the potatoes start to brown. (Don't brown them too much. Remember you will be baking them on a pizza later.)

To prepare pizza: Preheat oven (preferably a wood-fired oven) to 500°F. Place your pizza dough on a floured smooth surface. Form a pizza by using your fingertips to stretch the dough. Transfer dough to a pizza stone or pan.

Brush garlic oil lightly over pizza dough (leaving about ¼ inch of dough—"the crust"—untouched by garlic oil around entire pizza). Sprinkle rosemary evenly over oiled part of pizza dough. Spread garlic paste evenly over oiled part of pizza.

Spread shredded fontina cheese evenly on pizza dough, leaving "the crust" untouched. Place goat cheese evenly over shredded fontina cheese. Place sliced Yukon Gold potatoes evenly, covering the fontina cheese and goat cheese.

Bake for about 15–18 minutes or until the crust is golden brown and the cheese is completely melted. Cut into eight slices. Garnish with wild arugula and a drizzle of white truffle oil. Serve and enjoy!

Pizza

While we only include one pizza shop in this book, there are actually many favorites around town.

Maxwell's New York–style crust entices those from the East Coast as well as the West, and their Fat Kid pizza topped with ricotta, spinach, and pepperoni will put a smile on anyone's face.

Settebello is known for its Napoletana pizza, a traditional Italian-style pie, enjoyed best with just a few toppings.

Locals love Este Pizza, which offers takeout plus gluten-free and vegan options. The Italian Flag specialty pie is one to remember.

Vinto specializes in unique pizzas like the Patate, with Yukon Gold potatoes and truffle oil, and the Tutabella, with house-made sausage and peppers. They also offer specials and seasonal pizzas as well as gluten-free crust.

And The Pie, we can't forget The Pie—deep-dish pizza so thick and dense you only need one piece, but so good you'll probably have two.

Flatbread Neapolitan Pizzeria in Sugarhouse serves up the classics with a touch of local taste, such as their Capricciosa and Diavola with Creminelli meats, which are best enjoyed on their patio.

For calzones, Roasted Sun Pizzeria and Nuch's both have great options.

WILD GRAPE

481 EAST SOUTH TEMPLE
SALT LAKE CITY, UTAH 84111
(801) 746-5565
WILDGRAPEBISTRO.COM
JUAN CARLOS, HEAD CHEF
TROY AND JESSICA GREENHAWT, OWNERS

Troy and Jessica Greenhawt moved into the Avenues Bakery location months after Kathie Chadbourne moved her operation deeper into the throws of the Avenues. After a quick turnaround they opened as Wild Grape in 2009 with an award-winning bartender, Sean Neves (now of Church and State fame), a storied chef in Phelix Gardner (now at Scott Evans's establishments Finca and Pago), and a measure of goodwill from the community.

Yes, we're kind of name-dropping a bit here. Wild Grape is the perfect illustration of the small SLC food and beverage scene interweaving. Chefs bounce around from restaurant to restaurant. They're a nomadic people. Bartenders follow suit. So with every great restaurant and chef comes the influence of another great restaurant and chef.

Current head chef Juan Carlos started washing dishes in the Wild Grape kitchen and learned from some of the talented chefs, most notably Phelix. Juan Carlos joined Phelix at various other endeavors for a stint, eventually finding his way back to Troy's

kitchen, where the two work closely as head chef and general manager. These two collaborate and support each other on everything from what's on the menu to the kitchen staff.

For Juan Carlos the reward for his time, effort, and passion is simply when someone enjoys his food. If you see his smiling face walking through the restaurant, stop him and tell him what you enjoyed about your food.

While the legacy of past chefs remain, the vibrance of Juan Carlos's demeanor is now what gives Wild Grape's kitchen its energy.

Pork Chop & Beer Sauce

(SERVES 4)

For the pork chops:

4 (1½-inch-thick) bone-in pork chops (preferably from the rib end)
2 teaspoons salt
2 teaspoons coarsely ground pepper
½ cup olive oil

For the beer pan sauce:

6 tablespoons butter
2 large shallots (about 1 cup), diced
4 tablespoons brown sugar, packed
2 tablespoons Dijon mustard
2 cups Uinta Dubhe Black IPA (you may use Guinness, Anchor Bock, or your favorite dark beer)
2 teaspoons fresh thyme leaves

To prepare pork chops: Heat a large sauté pan over medium-high heat for 2 minutes or until very hot. Sprinkle one side of each pork chop with salt and pepper. Add the olive oil to the pan and then place the chops in the pan, seasoned side down. Sprinkle the rest of the salt and pepper over the top of the chops. While the pork is cooking, prep the ingredients for the pan sauce. When the bottom of the chops are a nice golden brown, 3–4 minutes, flip them over and cook the other side for 3–4 minutes for medium; thicker chops will be medium-rare. Transfer to a plate and let the chops rest while you make the sauce. Tent the chops with foil while resting if you want them more well done.

To prepare beer pan sauce: Heat the same pan to high heat and add the butter, swirling to melt. Add the shallots and stir, scraping up all the bits from the bottom of the pan. Sauté the shallots for 2 minutes or until golden and translucent. Add the brown sugar and whisk to melt. Add the Dijon mustard and whisk again. Add the beer and fresh thyme leaves. Cook the sauce for 1 minute, whisking while the sauce gently boils. This will help thicken the sauce. Turn the heat off.

To serve: Transfer the chops to a serving platter and spoon beer pan sauce over the top. Serve the remaining sauce on the side. Plate with your favorite vegetables and/or potatoes.

Quantity is perhaps the poorest measure of quality. Utah's breweries may be few, but no drop is wasted on substandard swill. Don't let the number of local microbreweries fool you; Utah's bars and breweries boast damn good beer. And don't let the 3.2 percent ABW limitation on grocery store beer get you down. A beer overlooked due to low alcohol content only shows the ignorance of the consumer and offers no commentary on the beer itself. In the same way that a larger number of breweries in Utah does little to validate the existing breweries, so does higher alcohol. Good beer has always been about one thing: good beer.

The state of beer in Utah is good and is swinging ever upward, but only after decades of significant downturn. For there to have been downturn means that at one point, breweries in Utah enjoyed a surprising heyday. Ironically, at one time Utah housed one of the largest breweries in the United States, Salt Lake City Brewing, owned and operated by Jacob Moritz. The Mormon faith once allowed consumption of alcohol for worthy members of the church, and thus a few early breweries were owned and supported by Mormons. In 1921 the LDS church made adherence to the Word of Wisdom necessary for Temple entry, ending the period of feast for the local brewing industry. Surprisingly, Utah voted to repeal Prohibition in December 1933. Its vote was the last needed to pass the measure. High West celebrates Utah's contribution to the end of Prohibition with a barrel-aged Manhattan appropriately named The 36th Vote.

Post-Prohibition and Word of Wisdom limitations in the market presented challenges that were eventually insurmountable. In 1967 Fisher Brewing, the only brewery in Utah at the time, closed its doors, beginning a prohibition of a different style for the next nineteen years.

WASATCH BREWING

Enter Greg Schirf. He paved the way and opened the doors for the scene that locals enjoy so much now. Greg worked to legalize the brewpub concept already prevalent elsewhere by working with a senator from Price, Utah, of all places. The opening of Schirf Brewing Company (eventually Wasatch Brewing) marked the end of a nineteen-year drought in brewing on Utah soil.

Wasatch formed a cooperative with Squatters Pub Brewery in 2000, called the Utah Brewers Cooperative, which eventually led to combining their breweries and bottling operations at 1763 South 300 West. While both maintain their respective brands and brews, everything else operates under one roof.

RED ROCK BREWING

Thanks to Schirf's efforts, Red Rock Brewing began as a brewpub in the heart of downtown near the convention center, where it enjoys a packed house on a regular basis. In 2000 *Brewpub Magazine* named Red Rock the brewpub of the year, memorializing a change in Utah in front of the national scene. To boot, the Great American Beer Festival named Red Rock the Large Brewpub of the Year in 2007. Not only does Utah have brewpubs, but they're also the best brewpubs in the country.

After enjoying more than a hundred awards for its in-house brews, Red Rock made the jump out of the house and started bottling high-point beers, something the brewpub could never offer thanks to the 3.2 restrictions. Among some pretty incredible bottled beer, the Elephino scored an 87 by *Beer Advocate* and continually proves to be a favorite among hops lovers in Salt Lake.

UINTA

In 1993 Uinta Brewing started brewing beers exclusively for wholesale. With no designs on a brewpub or restaurant, Uinta pushed hard to make Utah proud by brewing consistently good 3.2 beer. Walk the massive brewing facility in Salt Lake and you'll be blown away that something of this size is still called a "micro" brewery. But owner Steve Kuftinec is quick to point out that Coors Brewing produces more in one day than Uinta produces in a year.

Uinta became something that had not existed since the early years of the twentieth century: a significant brewery that makes waves beyond Utah's borders. Inside Utah, the famous Cutthroat Pale Ale has, since the beginning, been the best-selling Uinta beer. But beyond our borders, the Hop Nosh (formerly Hop Notch) put Utah on the radar of IPA enthusiasts around the country. In 2013 Hop Nosh surpassed Cutthroat for the first time as Uinta's best seller.

EPIC BREWING

Epic Brewing came on the brewing scene and proved that high-point beer in Utah is a successful model for making highly desirable beer and plenty of money. All Epic brews are twenty-two-ounce high-point beers meant to be shared with a friend or finished after a long day.

There are some pretty clear limitations with Epic's model that should have certainly led to their demise. First, only 3.2 beer can be sold in grocery stores. Most people buy beer at the grocery store. That's a clear advantage to breweries like Uinta that do 3.2 really well. Second, the bottles are huge by comparison to the standard twelve-ounce bottles that normally define the single-serving size. And third, they're new to a market with a lot of loyalty to the present breweries.

In the face of these few disadvantages, Epic sold out of their entire production the first week they were open, quickly proving that Utah's pulse is changing. Epic's success most clearly tells the story of Utah as it exists today. The total number of beer drinkers is on the rise, and they are willing to pay more for beer and drink beer at higher points.

Every brewery in some way shows the pioneer spirit of Utah. Each one offers something just different enough to build a fan base to support itself. From the days of Moritz and Salt Lake Brewing to Schirf's pioneering work and the reawakening of Utah's once massive beer scene, the condition of beer in Utah is strong.

Index

About the Authors

Josh Rosenthal left West Texas as soon as he could for the mountains of Northern Utah, but he made sure to lure the lovely Becky Burns to come along after her four years at the University of Oklahoma. Through a series of miracles, Becky chose Josh and together they became the Rosenthals.

Josh lives as a singer/songwriter/ author/pastor/entrepreneur supporting Becky in her endeavors with Grace Food Group (Vintage Mixer, a recipe blog focusing on seasonal, fresh ingredients, and SLC Foodie). Josh is also the CEO of Charming Beard Coffee Roasters, a small local roaster with two locations in Salt Lake City and more than sixty wholesale accounts. You'll also find him as an associate pastor at Missio Dei Community in downtown Salt Lake City. In all of their efforts, Josh and Becky seek the best for Salt Lake City and the people who choose to call it home. However, the adventure of transcontinental travel constantly catches their imagination leading to excessive daydreaming and scheming of their next trip abroad.

HEIDI LARSEN OF FOODIECRUSH

Josh and Becky live in Salt Lake City with their son Everett and Portuguese waterdog, Henry. They are the driving forces behind a few popular blogs for foodies in Salt Lake City. Check out SLCfoodie.com for local food info, @SLCfoodie on Twitter, or theVintageMixer.com.